Tami -

Sometimes we fr[illegible]
ourselves beating do[illegible]
before we can break thro[illegible]

Enjoy -

Stacy Pawels

Empty Cupboards
Essays

An analysis of the breakdown of a commonsensical, menopausing Leo, living in high altitude where oxygen is scant

Stacey Powells

ISBN: 979-8-9863858-8-4 (Paperback)
ISBN: 979-8-9863858-9-1 (eBook)
Library of Congress Control Number application submitted

Dangling Participle Press
Mammoth Lakes, California
www.danglingparticiplepress.com

Book design: Lisa Lucca and JohnEdgar.design

Many names were changed in these stories to protect their privacy…and mine.

"Once upon a time I was falling in love,
now I'm only falling apart.
Nothing I can do,
total eclipse of the heart."

–Jim Steinman, "Total Eclipse of The Heart"

For those humans who never imagined you would fall apart
… but you did.

Contents

Introduction

I had a bad day for eighteen months, and because I didn't have a gun in the house, I am here today to write about most of it. It wasn't just one occurrence that sent me down the black brick road into the land of antidepressants and therapists; an accumulation of events since I was in single digits all added up to the big brain *kaboom*.

Before my mental health did a one-eighty, I was one of those people who—when told so-and-so was having a very hard time with depression or anxiety—would tell the person to "get over it," or "go for a walk, meditate, do yoga, or take a road trip."

And then it happened to me.

I was the one trippin'. At the peak of my brain disability, when I could not function, smelling for days was the norm. Going away or taking a meditation class did not work. All the shit going around in my head was still there wherever I went.

It was as if my higher power wanted to make sure I truly understood depression and didn't treat it as an afterthought. The only way I could grasp the enormity of a malfunctioning brain was to become someone who experienced cheerlessness and despondency and the inability to get out of bed for days.

I. Had. A. Nervous . . . *What?*

By definition, the word "nervous" means, "To be highly excitable; unnaturally or acutely uneasy. Apprehensive." I could have been suffering from disordered nerves. But what happened to my brain was not disordered, nor did I feel nervous. I took a full-blown mental nosedive. A spiral descent into the unfamiliar. A rupturing of improbable proportions. In other words, I fucking cracked up.

We've all seen those slow-motion photos on television showing what the Big Bang must have looked like when our universe was created, or what the sun looks like when it sends a solar flare out into the universe.

That was me.

The good daughter/friend/student/wife/mother image I had carried along for decades exploded into bits and pieces, fracturing off into parts unknown.

After forty-ish years, my brain had had enough. Much like how an oversaturated mountainside slumps and slips, destroying everything in its path, my mental state slurped all over itself, losing all sense of direction and purpose.

The following stories have been tugged and heaved and yanked from my memory. They reflect specific moments that may or may not have contributed to the mental breakdown which was not supposed to happen, but it did and inevitably subsidized the girl/woman/friend/wife/mother I had become.

All the people over the years who crossed my path helped to shape me. They may have rejected me, screwed me, loved me, raised me, judged me, taunted me, disregarded me, or honored me, but they are all part of my story. After a lifetime in the making, I'm now telling it out loud for all the humans who fell apart and out of themselves. This is for those who have tried so hard to put themselves back together without letting anyone know—piece by fucking piece.

These essays are mostly from before the big brain blowout, but some are from after, because the tentacles of my mental health breakdown are still alive and well, always testing and prodding, hoping for an encore. I still have moments when I'm terrified and can't function past the next five minutes, let alone the next five days. That's when I go into self-care mode. On those days, I'm so grateful for the husband I now have. He holds me tight or leaves me alone or lets me venture off for days or weeks to get my head straight again without judgment, emotional chaos, or guilt.

These are stories about silence and strength, stupidity and awkwardness, abuse and denial, resilience and apathy. They are based on my truth of what happened to me, but please keep in mind, I am a post-menopausal, creative Leo, with an overactive memory. I am also a woman who comes from a long line of women known to keep emotions pushed down until there is nowhere else for them to go but up and out and all over the place.

Everything I thought I was and who I was supposed to be broke out of their respective molds, leaving me feeling like one of those gurgling mud pots you see when visiting Yellowstone National Park, empty as soon as the gasses bellow into thin air.

This book is a path of discovery, trying to find out why I had become a woman who fell apart. A woman who sang "Total Eclipse of the Heart" over and over again whenever she decided to take a shower.

A woman who … wasn't.

My hope is that whoever reads this will know they are not alone in this eccentric, bizarre, and peculiar world where crazy shit happens to everyone. No one is spared. It takes a network of love and compassion to sustain what it means to be human these days, and I have been graced with the most extraordinary soul-sister network.

You know who you are.

Without all of you…well, let's not go there.

The Roof

I've been reading about the side effects of frontal lobe injuries and wonder if I sustained brain damage when I fell off the roof.

From 1964 until 1972, we lived on Sylvan Street in Reseda, California. Reseda is a suburb in the San Fernando Valley, which in turn, is a suburb of the greater Los Angeles area. The house was the first that my parents purchased after living in an apartment building owned by my grandmother Toby, my mother's mother. I know my dad wasn't keen on living above his mother-in-law, but she did help them out when he was still going to school, working full-time, and about to be a father to me, their happy accident.

It was a three-bedroom home with a large backyard, a screened-in porch, and a den where my dad would sometimes play his percussion instruments while my mom danced to Sergio Mendes and Brasil '66.

The backyard consisted of a large red-brick patio surrounding a huge maple tree. Every fall, my father spent hours sweeping and raking the leaves, causing more than a few expletives to leave his mouth.

The year was 1969. I was ten and the oldest of three children. It was Saturday, April 5th, the day before Easter—an exciting day because it meant our family would load up in our blue station wagon and make the drive over to the Westside of Los Angeles to our paternal grandparents' home on Easter Sunday.

We didn't think about the millions of people around the world who would hike at sunrise to a cross. Instead, Easter Sunday meant we got to play with our cousins, eat meals surrounded by loved ones, and search for dyed eggs. We were a weird non-Jewish/Jewish family who used every holiday celebrated by every religion known as a reason for the twelve of us, our core family, to get together.

On that Saturday, I was playing Frisbee on the patio and my parents were inside. I know it was late in the afternoon because my father worked at his pharmacy on Saturdays from 9:00 A.M. until 3:00 P.M. If he was home it was because his workday was over. Whoever was throwing the Frisbee with me, most likely my five-year-old brother, was pretty bad, because it flew over my head and landed on the roof of our one-story home.

Unlike most kids who would yell for their parents, I decided to climb the ladder and get the Frisbee myself. A ladder was leaning against the roof right near where it had landed. I'd seen my dad climb onto the roof a number of times. Piece of cake.

I climbed up the ladder and looked down at whoever had thrown the Frisbee up there in the first place. I grabbed it, threw it down, and then everything went black. Next thing I knew, my father was picking up my Raggedy Ann body and putting me into our station wagon. My mother was crying. I had no idea what my siblings were doing. Maybe my mother called Winnie Kettles, our neighbor, to come over and watch them while she and my dad drove me to the hospital. I slipped in and out of consciousness.

Dad drove me to the closest emergency room, which was Encino Hospital. However, after I was stabilized, I was transferred to Queen of Angels Hospital near downtown Los Angeles. It had something to do with the type of medical insurance we had at the time. My parents transported me. They couldn't afford an ambulance bill while they were still paying off my father's college loans.

When I asked my mom what she remembered about that day, it turned out that her memory of the event differed slightly from mine.

"Wasn't the ladder in the front of the house?" she asked.

"No, Mom. The brick patio was in the backyard."

"Oh, right. Your dad and I were in the living room and he happened to turn at the exact time you fell off the roof. He was terrified." It must have been traumatic for him, seeing his daughter slam her head onto a brick patio.

Falling off our roof on April 5, 1969 meant I missed Easter Sunday at my grandparents' home. I was more upset about not seeing my cousins than I was about my broken wrist or the concussion. My parents and siblings visited me afterward with a big basket of chocolate eggs, which the doctor immediately took away because you're not supposed to eat chocolate after having a concussion.

The fall from our roof still affects me to this day. Fifty years later, my skin has thinned, and the area where my head slammed onto the brick patio has become more pronounced. Above my right eye is a knot the size of a grape. People watch me on Zoom and ask if a spider bit me in the middle of the night. Just like Lauren Hutton has a big gap in between her front teeth and Angelina Jolie has full, natural lips, and Jimmy Durante had a large nose, the skull knot above my right eye is my own signature physical characteristic, a reminder of the concussion when my head met brick.

I also found out I have a piece of floating bone in my right wrist, the one that absorbed the initial impact when I fell onto the brick patio. After a pickleball faux pas, I had to have my wrist X-rayed, and the orthopedic doc asked if I had ever broken it before, because there was a very old, worn-down piece of bone floating around and messing with some of the nerves in the area where the wrist connects to my right hand. Whoever the doctor had been back in 1969 should have taken a closer look at the X-ray. Apparently, a piece of my bone chipped off and they never saw it so it's been floating around in there for over fifty years, just waiting for the right pickleball wrist-flip-move to set it off.

I wonder what the statute of limitations is on something like this. Then again, the Queen of Angels Hospital has not existed for decades. Scientologists bought the building sometime in the 1980s.

The frontal lobe, where the concussion took place, is the most important area of the brain for a variety of human skills, such as rationalizing and language. Is the reason I now struggle with words due to the damage my frontal lobe sustained when I fell off that roof at the age of ten? Was my mental breakdown in 2001 a delayed reaction of the head crash? How many straws can I grasp at one time?

The frontal lobes are also the last part of the brain to mature. Did the concussion slow down my reasoning abilities? Damage to the frontal lobe can affect attention and concentration skills. I must say, the older I become the less I can concentrate on certain things. When I had my breakdown I couldn't concentrate on anything at all. I had to mark on my calendar the days I showered so if a few days passed, I knew I had to bathe.

Another side effect of the concussion was the memory recall I had several months later. I used to ride horses at Foxfield Riding Academy in Westlake Village, California. My mother related a story to me where during one lesson, I had fallen off my horse and gotten hysterical. Falling off the horse was no big deal because that's a part of riding English and jumping over fences. Sometimes you fall off the horse. What was a big deal was that no one was able to calm me down, and they had to remove me and the horse from the riding arena.

My mother figured out I was re-experiencing the roof fall because up until then, I couldn't remember tumbling off our roof.

I could only remember being on the roof and then being carried by my dad to our blue station wagon.

If a fall from a horse triggered the trauma of my falling off the roof, then what combination of events triggered my meltdown in 2001?

I Should Have

I was twelve and swimming in the Santa Monica Bay when I was grabbed from behind. Decades later, I remember everything about him. His skin was the same color as the crayon in my 1970s box called Sepia. He had short, black hair, a wiry mustache, and after he pinched my left breast, he laughed a sick saltwater laugh between the swells that were making their way toward the beach. His voice was throaty and gurgling, and I wanted a shark to yank him under the dirty Pacific so the sound coming from his face would drown with the rest of him.

I snapped my head toward the shore. Too far. I was behind where the waves crested and broke, barely making out the pink and purple of my mother's beach umbrella, which seemed muted under the foggy Los Angeles sky.

They were too far away. Everyone was too far away.

I tried to wipe the seawater off my face and out of my eyes. I took a quick look back at the stranger who had just …

Mom! Where are you? Help me!

I stared at him for a moment, wondering what I should do because I knew what he'd done was very wrong. The swells continued to lift us up and down, up and down. My feet never touched the sandy bottom and I kicked desperately to stay afloat. His lecherous face smirked, then broke into a repulsive grin when another swell pushed him inches closer. Kicking away as hard as I could, I felt sick to my stomach as my big toe swept across his hairy belly. He sneered, exposing a mouth of rotted teeth. I wanted to scream but the sound of the ocean between us and the shore was too loud. And if I screamed, he could have been on me in two quick strokes, pushing my head underwater, making sure I never screamed again. Nobody would have heard my voice over the sound of the waves crashing around us. I prayed for a riptide to sweep me fast and far, but prayers aren't always answered when you need them most.

His back was to the vast Pacific. He glanced quickly over my shoulder toward the beach, then turned to face me again, a sickening look of triumph on his pockmarked face. His expression of conquest is embedded in my memory forever. This was new territory for my adolescent brain. My mother always told me not to talk to strangers, but she never told me about the depraved humans I might meet while swimming in the ocean. I was so scared.

I glanced behind him. A series of swells piled up, one after the other. It was as though one of my angels decided to finally intervene, and I watched with relief as one of the swells grew and peaked behind the man. I turned fast and hard, catching the look of surprise on his face as he got pounded by the same wave that carried me back to the safety of shallow water, far away from the first man who ever touched my breast. I hope he drowned or broke his neck so he wouldn't be able to touch any more little girls.

I never told anyone what happened.

My best friend, Nina, was with me at the beach that day. She was a rebellious tween whose purpose in life was to do everything her over-protective parents told her not to do. Nina always had a glint in her eye, which years later I would recognize as the precursor to a lie she was about to tell, usually about having sex with someone she pretended to know. She was also a narcissist. If I had told her about my brush with molestation, she would have pretended to be concerned for a few minutes, then would have found some way to make it all about her. She would have wished she was the one who had her preteen breast pinched by a stranger with rotten teeth behind the waves.

The year was 1972. On that summer day, when the fog held steady over the Santa Monica Bay like a blanket wrapped tightly around a newborn, I decided that telling anyone about my behind-the-waves encounter, even the lifeguard, would be embarrassing.

But I should have.

I thought it better to forget about my first brush with molestation. The jelly-like part of my hypothalamus does a great job of helping me remember and forget historical events from my life, good and bad. I put my molestation incident neatly into the memory compartment I kept specifically for the perverts who have crossed my path over the years. Until now, no one else knew about that day.

Like the good and responsible girl I was, I body surfed my way back to safety, crawled up to my beach towel, and fell face-first onto the terry cloth pattern of yellow happy faces. I was very still, counting how many times my heart thumped before it slowed to an unnoticeable rhythm, helping me forget that some disgusting stranger grabbed at my chest offshore in the Pacific Ocean. I carried on my perfect beach day, pretending my innocence had not been disrupted. I didn't disturb the peace. I made sure my world continued to run smoothly underneath the calm, gray-sky.

Maybe my "should have's" began that day.

Or maybe they started a month earlier, when a relative reached around me and pinched my breast when we were all swimming in my grandpa's pool. I never told anyone about that incident either.

I should have screamed both times.

I should have told the lifeguard at the beach.

I should have told my mother everything.

Reseda, the Walnut, the Piggly Wiggly and Candy

Until I was eleven, I grew up in the flatlands of the San Fernando Valley town made famous by Tom Petty singing about free falling and being a bad boy for breaking some poor girl's heart. It was a place where my mom was able to breeze into a drive-through dairy in our blue Dodge wagon to pick up milk, and it was the place where I didn't understand why people made fun of our family because we celebrated all holidays. It was where my parents had their first argument with neighbors down the street, and the kitchen in that Reseda house is where I came home from school one afternoon and asked my Grandma Bess if she was a slut.

I stood in the doorway between the dining room and kitchen. My mother and my grandmother were standing at the sink talking. My little brother was sitting in the corner of our kitchen table underneath the window shoving Cheerios into his mouth. I had my Barbie lunchbox in one hand, and my favorite orange fuzzy sweater in the other. The smell of something floury and sweet was coming from the oven, and my dog Candy was scratching at the back door because she had heard me come home from school. She was the same dog my parents later gave away because they thought I was allergic to her. I was, but they had no clue it was also the smoke from the three packs a day my mother smoked that sent me repeatedly to the emergency room. Kent cigarettes. Just the name makes my mouth go dry.

"Grandma? Are you a slut?"

She looked down at me, then at my mother, and then back at me. She turned her body so she was facing me and put her hands on her hips. "What did you just say to me?!"

I had obviously heard the word *slut* at the elementary school I attended around the corner from our house. How was I to know it was one of the bad words? I was only six or seven. It was, however, one of those words that made my mother take a backhand to my right cheek.

"You apologize to your grandmother this instant!" Mom grabbed my arm and tugged, yanking me hard until I was standing directly in front of Grandma Bess. "Now!"

I never said the word again for a long time afterward, and it wasn't until years later that I found out what it meant. I wish I could ask Grandma Bess how I apologized, but unfortunately, some years back she joined my dad wherever our souls go when they are done being down here on Earth.

The Reseda years were a tapestry of good times and bad. Getting up early every Saturday morning to go horseback riding was a joy but that feeling was extinguished one weekend when my little brother set fire to my large, stuffed dog who I had named Stanley.

We always looked forward to Mom driving us to Zuma Beach during the summer with some of the neighborhood kids. One Sunday in particular she wanted to leave extra early which was peculiar because she rarely got us all packed and in the car before eleven. It all became clear when we came home only to find that my dad cut down my favorite tree in our front yard. They had conspired to keep me away from the house all day knowing I would protest the demolition of my tree who I had named Queen Maple.

Having a candy party at our Reseda home every Halloween became a tradition, but when the Sylmar quake struck at six in the morning on February 9, 1971, knocking my English riding hardhat off the shelf and onto my head, our Reseda days were numbered. That next summer we moved from the flatlands of the San Fernando Valley up into a community tucked away into the canyons of the Santa Monica Mountains.

Decades later the smell of antiseptic and first aid lotion reminds me of when I smashed my big toe on a neighbor's porch. I was probably ten, bouncing up and down on my Hippity-Hop, then flipped backwards while going down a set of cement stairs, smashing my big toe. I did things like that. Very tomboy-esque.

Reseda is where I'd play the *Jesus Christ Superstar* soundtrack over and over, driving my mother and siblings mad by singing the words to, "I Don't Know How to Love Him," at the top of my prepubescent and asthmatic lungs. It was also where I heard that a bunch of school girls were going to "scrub" me for entering the seventh grade at Sequoia Junior High School. Thankfully, our move to Encino in the summer of 1971 prevented me from enduring that humiliation. Scrubbing was a rite-of-passage for kids entering junior high school for the first time, and usually involved things like getting mashed potatoes dumped on your head during lunch or being held down while a bunch of girls smothered your face with lipstick.

I wasn't beaten or abused. As a matter of fact, I had a decent childhood. I was raised by my stay-at-home mom and pharmaceutical dad. I did well in school and had lots of friends. But little moments of angst have stuck with me all these years. Maybe it was a mistake to hold on to them. Did the Reseda years start the breakup of my mental composure?

There was the time I went to the store with our neighbor. Apparently, this neighbor forgot to tell my mother she was taking me, because when we got back home, a few police cars were out front waiting for us. My mother cried a lot that day and made me promise at least a hundred times never to go anywhere with a stranger. The lady who took me was our next-door neighbor. We all knew her. She wasn't a stranger but after that day, she wasn't even a friend.

Embarrassing my mother at the Piggly Wiggly in Reseda is my earliest recollection of feeling ashamed.

"What's in your hand?" she asked as she was putting away the groceries in the back of the station wagon. It was the kind of car with a back window that rolled up automatically when my mom pressed the button.

"Nothing," I replied. She waited until she put all the groceries away, shutting the tailgate and rolling up the electric window with her car key. Then she turned on me fast, pried my hand open, revealing the walnut I had taken from the store.

"It's just a walnut, Mom. What's the big deal?!"

In an instant, I was being dragged through the parking lot. My mother's nails were digging into my flesh, and she went on a rant about thievery and stealing and jail.

"Do you want to go to jail?! Well? Do you?" She was relentless. "You'll be away from your cousins and your grandparents and you will bring shame to your family! Your friends won't ever come over again and you won't be invited to anyone's party! Is that what you want? Is it?"

The manager didn't press charges, and I sure didn't steal anything again for a long time afterward.

The walnut incident may have been the same day my mother had a meltdown on the Ventura Freeway. She didn't have meltdowns often, but when she did, it was all or nothing. My siblings were fighting in the back seat, and instead of turning around and yelling at them for the umpteenth time, my mother pulled over on the side of the freeway, got out of the car, and started walking. Right there on the 101 freeway between the exits for Hayvenhurst Avenue and Balboa Boulevard, she took a stroll.

My heart pounded and my breath caught in my throat. I felt a stress-induced asthma attack developing in my chest. Just as quickly as the back-seated offspring had started their squabble, they stopped, looking wide-eyed as our mother walked away from us on the Ventura Freeway with cars whooshing past.

The air in the station wagon was thick with city-desert heat, and I was sure we were going to suffocate in our own shock. Mothers don't do that. Mothers don't abandon their kids while driving anywhere, let alone on the Ventura Freeway. But ours did. She had had enough. She'd reached her end zone and made her point without saying another word about it when she finally got back into the car. She was gone only ten minutes, which seemed like forever to a twelve-year-old.

I learned a valuable lesson that day. Decades later, I did the same thing to my kids when they were fighting, except we were not on the freeway. We were on some long and windy narrow mountain road in the Cascades near Mt. Lassen. My kids were fighting because they were sick of being stuck in the car together for days on end. Or were they fighting because once again their dad decided at the last minute not to go on a road trip with his family and that's just what the two-man swam, my boys, did every day? Doesn't matter. The result was me jerking the car over to the side of the road, getting out, and stomping into the forest, saying nothing to my boys. I moved far enough away so I could no longer hear them trying to get me back by honking the car horn.

I might still be in the forest today had it not been for the swarm of hornets that found me as I sat down heavily on a tree stump. When I returned, my boys were subdued. The ride to the next town was very quiet. As we pulled into the parking lot of a roadside café, it was my elder son who spoke first.

"Moms aren't supposed to leave their kids alone in the car. No mom ever does that," he said, pouting a little, his lower lip quivering a lot. *Little does he know*, I thought to myself.

Reseda days meant the Helms Bakery truck would roll slowly down the street playing jingle songs that brought us all to the curb for hot, fresh donuts and pastries. Those donuts, undoubtedly, slowly adding to my hefty physique. Back then, parents didn't know, or didn't care, what too much sugar did to our bodies.

I wasn't thinking about the Reseda years when I finally took the mental plunge, but our unique personal histories stay somewhere close by. They prickle through occasionally, reminding us of how our past can shape the people we become.

Was it the neighbor who lived across the street being friendly one day and hating us the next that added to my rupture years later, in 2001? Or was it the father of one of my friends who got a little too close to my crotch with his hand as he helped me into the saddle of their horse? He never moved his hand as I sat on the saddle until I kicked the horse to move. I'm still creeped out thinking about his hand being where it shouldn't have been. Perhaps that's when my internal switch began to flip. Or was it when I was holding on tight to the fur of my dog as my parents pulled her away from me?

Everything about the moment they gave my dog Candy away is as clear as if it had just happened yesterday. I was sitting on the brick patio in our backyard right under our maple tree. I was brushing Candy's fur when a stranger came into the yard with my parents in tow. My chest caved and I gulped air in between an exacerbated crying jag as they hooked an unfamiliar leash to her blue collar, pulling her from my grasp. I was devastated.

My knees started to bleed as I was being dragged over the brick patio toward the driveway along with my dog. My mother, or maybe it was my father, grabbed me around the waist and pried my fingers free from German shepherd fur. My blue dress got dirty. My white patent leather shoes were no longer white. The bow that was once threaded neatly through my braids hung limply around the bottom of my hair and for the first time in my life I felt hatred toward my parents.

The entire episode eventually became part of the *back then* file I stashed away somewhere. *Back then*, you weren't supposed to make your little sister ride on the back of your classic Schwinn Stingray bike with the banana seat and sissy bar, because you knew she was too young to know how to hold on and not fall off, resulting in her finger caught in the spokes. *Back then*, smoking cigarettes in the car while your kids were in the backseat with the windows rolled up wasn't frowned upon by more than half the nation.

Back then, you weren't supposed to hate your parents.

Murrieta Hot Springs

In the late 1960s and early 1970s, my mother and her mother took us once a year to Murrieta Hot Springs, a resort near the town of Temecula, where many families from Los Angeles fled to get away from city life. My father never went with us. He preferred high altitude, choosing the Sierra Nevada Mountains for his escapes. Besides, he rarely left his Beverly Hills pharmacy for more than a week. What would his celebrity clients do without him and their legal/semi-legal backdoor drug exchanges?

In the center of a very large swimming pool at Murrieta was a huge mosaic mushroom. The tiles on the mushroom were pink, turquoise, and white, with a spray of water flying out the top, making raindrop noises as the droplets hit the pool. Kids of all colors, shapes, and sizes scrambled to reach the top, then dove off the ceramic fungus into the crystal blue, overly chlorinated water.

I was a preteen when, one summer, I dove into the pool from the mushroom and came up with the top half of my bathing suit floating some five feet away. It was black with little yellow fish splayed about, and the bottom half of the suit cut into the sides of my hips, leaving mean red marks on my skin. I told my mom many times I needed a new swimsuit, but she only muttered something about my father having a rough time at the pharmacy, and that maybe I should think about cutting down on my french fry consumption.

My birthday was in the middle of summer, and I should have had a new swimsuit that year. My top popping off in the pool was proof my preteen body was changing. My clothing needed to be re-evaluated. Mom had ignored my plea.

Panicked, I glanced around the pool to make sure no one saw the swath of fabric floating in the water. I couldn't touch the bottom and had to kick extra hard to make it to my bathing suit top. The frenetic water ripples made by my mad attempt to get to it as fast as possible pushed it farther away from me. My arms were crossed over my chest, so it was only the force of my legs and body trying to snag the top. Back then I would have never thought to just saunter over, topless, grab the suit, and glare at anyone who dared to look. I wasn't as brave as I pretended to be. I wanted to be brave like my neighbor, Shirley, who went to Woodstock and danced naked on the grass with thousands of people. At least that's the story she told me the last time she was our babysitter.

But Murrieta wasn't Woodstock.

As I made an awkward attempt to try to retrieve my floating top, I did not see the shadow under the water speeding toward me from the other direction until it was too late. A hand broke the surface and pulled the piece of fabric under, then swam away another ten feet or so before the drenched, red head of a teenage boy popped up, his hand holding my top in the air like he had won the prize in a game of flag football. He guffawed at me, whistling loudly for the other kids in the pool to see what he had done, making fun of the half-naked little girl in the pool.

I screamed and screamed loud. "Mom! *Mom*!" It surprised me how loud I screamed for her. It was much louder than the boy's feeble attempt at humiliating me in the middle of the pool.

My mother, the fierce and bold Capricorn, flew off her lounge chair and was down the pool steps in seconds, chlorinated water spraying in all directions. In what seemed like three water-laden strides, her fingers planted themselves on the ears of the teenage villain and squeezed. He howled as he tried to get away, but my mother dragged him to where I was—hiding next to the mushroom, the cold tile pressing against my shoulders while I tried to shield my developing chest from the onlookers.

"Apologize to my daughter! Now!" bellowed my soft-spoken mother. The kid was close enough for me to see he hadn't brushed his teeth; there were black spots between his teeth and gums, like he had eaten a poppy seed muffin for breakfast. He had pimples down the right side of his face, and it was obvious one of his favorite pastimes was picking at them because several were scabbed over. His chest was sunken in and full of red splotches from too much sun.

He was still holding onto my bathing suit top, but after a final tug on his ear, he outstretched his arm. I looked at my mother in alarm. Did she really think I was going to uncross my chest to take it? Of course not. She snatched my top and simultaneously let go of the kid's ear, thrusting the top in my direction. I grabbed it from her and ducked down into the water.

As she started to walk toward the steps which led out of the pool, she came face to face with the father of the teenage hoodlum. They were both waist deep in the water. He loomed over my mother, as red in the face as his son.

"What the hell you doin' to my kid, lady?"

In the same voice she used when my little brother set something on fire, my mother screeched, "I'm teaching that boy of yours a lesson you have obviously yet to instill in your child!" The fight was on.

For a moment, the kid and I hid behind the mushroom, looking wide-eyed as our parents went at it. His dad was doing his best to intimidate my mother, who would have none of it. I was still standing cross-armed behind the mushroom, my bathing suit top stuffed in the crease between my upper arm and chest. I glanced to see if the red-haired teen was looking at me. He had disappeared, so I started to walk toward the pool steps. He reappeared moments later with a towel for me as I got out of the pool. He haphazardly draped it around my shoulders and mouthed an "I'm sorry" before ducking under the water to get away.

By the time I made it back to our lounge chairs, my mother was making her way across the pool back in my direction. She didn't say anything as she hastily gathered our belongings and shuffled me into the bathroom so I could take off the wet towel and put my top back on. The towel Red had brought me in the pool was soaking wet, and my mother handled it like she would a piece of trash about to get sent down the garbage chute, holding it out in front of her as she walked around the pool. The bottom of her sandals smacked the cement with the sucking sound of wet, cheap rubber. I watched in delighted horror as she dropped the wet towel onto the feet of Red's father, who was by then hidden behind a newspaper. He was startled out of his reading coma, and in his rustled state, got the bottom part of his legs stuck between the vinyl slats of the lounge chair. When he tried to stand up and untangle himself, the lounge chair flipped over and the father of Red stumbled onto the neighboring lounge chair, where one of his arms went through those vinyl slats as well. Red's dad cursed my mother and the world, and as she walked slowly toward me, a sly, all-knowing smile played at the corners of her lips.

I saw a different side of my mother that day. It had me curious about the woman who ran PTA meetings, took my sister to piano lessons, dropped my brother off at Little League practice, and drove me to horseback riding lessons.

Later that night, after our Murrieta Hot Springs dinner, my Grandma presented me with a big silver box wrapped in a pink ribbon. She handed it to me but didn't let go of the box. Instead, she and the box led me to the bed where she gingerly put it down, sitting next to it. She patted the bed. I sat next to her. I loved my mother's mother, my Grandma Toby. For no reason, out of the blue, she would present me or my sister or brother with something she wanted to buy us, "just because." As an adult, I know that's where I got my "just because" impulse to buy things for friends and family, even if it meant I would have to go two more weeks before being able to pay a bill. Friends and family are more important than bills.

I attacked the box as if it was my birthday all over again. But when I tore open the tissue paper and saw a frilly yellow dress with a pink sash, I became suspicious. The religious holidays I was obligated to attend weren't for several more months and as far as I knew, we weren't invited to any weddings or Bar Mitzvahs—especially at Murrieta Hot Springs.

"Do you like it, sweetie? It's for tonight," my grandmother whispered as she leaned toward me conspiratorially. The pearls around her neck clinked softly. I could smell her White Shoulders perfume. She glanced at my mother, who was sitting with her feet up on the other bed, combing out my sister's hair.

"What's happening tonight?" I asked. She turned her whole body around and faced my mother, astonished by the ignorance of her first born granddaughter.

"You mean you didn't tell her?" my grandmother said. I got that feeling in my stomach, the same one I got just before I had to take a math test.

"No, Ma. I thought I'd leave you that honor," answered my mother, not breaking her stride with the hairbrush, her tone flat like she was asking directions to the toilet paper aisle at the Piggly Wiggly. My sister was playing with a Barbie while my mother brushed her hair.

I assumed my sister wasn't paying attention to the conversation, since she has a history of having conversations in her head to which no one is privy. I was wrong. She was paying attention.

"Where's she going?" asked my sister, out of the blue, still moving the limbs of the Barbie this way and that.

"Yeah, where am I going?"

I caught the quick glare my grandmother sent across the room to my mother before she turned back to me and said, "Honey, you are going to your first dance tonight. Isn't it exciting?"

I looked at my mother, who continued brushing. I looked at my sister, who put her hand up to her mouth and giggled. I ran into the bathroom, shut the door, and cried until I made myself throw up.

It was a family dance not unlike those they have at family camps. I was grateful my grandmother and mother and sister were there because I was a nervous ninny. I was expected to dance with a boy. A *boy*! After the encounter with Red in the pool, I had had enough of boys.

The round tables were covered with white tablecloths and each seated ten. Various glasses filled with water and wine were scattered between plates of bread, salad, and roasted chicken. When I picked up the glass, it left a ring of water on the tablecloth. The six other people at our table were adults and kept to themselves. They got up to dance and then would come back to the table and drink. They knew one another, and I noticed they wouldn't always dance with the same partner. When I saw two of the women dancing together, I asked my mother why two women would dance with each other.

"Well, sometimes there just aren't enough men in the world, sweetie, and as women, we make do with what we have."

I was trying to be interested in the dolls my sister was playing with at our table when I felt a hand on my shoulder, light and tentative. Someone coughed behind me. I turned.

His black hair was pasted to his forehead with grease, and the sweat rings under his arm were brown around the edges. His eyes were a shimmering blue-gray and he sniffled constantly, wiping his nose on his sleeve. I saw him glance over to a corner where presumably his parents were in cahoots with my mother and grandmother. My grandmother had been coming to Murrieta for a long time, so it made sense she would be friendly with other regulars.

When I turned back around, he cleared his throat. My sister swiped at my shoulder and said, "There's a boy behind you hitting you on the back and making weird noises."

This was it. It was the boy the adults had chosen for my first real dance. He was older than me and was probably forced to come over and ask me to dance, just like I was forced to partake in my first dance wearing an obnoxious, frilly dress.

It really wasn't the first time I had been asked to dance with a boy. In the fourth grade, we had square dancing for P.E., and I had to do-si-do with other boys. But this wasn't square dancing. This was a real ballroom with a real band.

He bent his head close to my ear and said, "Look, I don't want to do this either, but my parents are making me and I guess they are making you too, so let's just do this and then you can go back to your dolls."

"They're not my dolls!" I shouted a bit too loudly. I shoved the chair back and marched onto the dance floor. My new dress made a swishing sound when I walked, and my black patent leather shoes hurt my toes. Just like my bathing suit, I had grown out of my shoes as well.

I was careful not to make eye contact with my mother, grandmother, or the dark-haired boy. I stood with my arms crossed in the middle of the dance floor amid men dancing with women, girls dancing with other boys, ladies dancing with ladies. The band was on a small stage in the corner and the music was some big band swing tune. People around us were shaking and twirling, lifting and bouncing. I didn't know how to properly dance and thankfully, neither did he. We stood on the floor, shuffling our feet, as awkward as two ducks in a swan pond, when he suddenly grabbed one of my hands, put the other on my shoulder, and said, "Just follow me." So there in the middle of a Benny Goodman song, we did the box step. Front step, sidestep, back step, sidestep, over and over again, until the music stopped.

It was just like I thought. My grandmother knew his parents, and the setup was for their enjoyment because neither Daniel (at least I found out his name) nor I was enjoying the dance. As he walked me back to the table with my sister and her dolls, my mother and his parents stopped us midway to take a picture. Minutes after I pulled out the chair to sit down again, there was another tap on my shoulder. I turned and stared open-mouthed at Red standing before me, all cleaned up.

"I was a jerk in the pool," he said.

"You said you were sorry. Thanks for the towel."

We stood there in uncomfortable silence. I could see through the sprouts of his red hair that the top of his head was sunburned. He smelled like bubble gum and mint and was making some kind of thwacking sound inside his mouth with his tongue. After a few seconds, Red finally looked down at me and shrugged.

"So, you wanna dance? I saw you dancing with the geek so I thought you would dance with me too."

"He's not a geek. He's a friend of … my grandma's." I looked to see where Daniel was standing, and Red followed my stare. Daniel was surrounded by a bunch of other boys who were all looking in my direction and snickering. Maybe he was a geek after all. And a jerk. I grabbed Red's hand and brazenly pulled him to the dance floor. I had my moments. The band began to play "Then He Kissed Me," originally recorded by The Crystals. I did my best to dance. So did Red.

"Did you get in trouble with your dad?" I asked.

"Nah, after he got through cussin' at your mom for dropping the towel on his legs, he said he did the same thing when he was a kid."

"Yeah, my mom was pretty mad at him."

"Not anymore," he whispered.

"Yes she is. She said that ..." But before I could finish my sentence, he was pointing behind me. I turned to see my mother, the woman who was married to my father, resting her head on the shoulder of Red's dad, laughing at something he whispered into her ear right then and there on the dance floor. She was wearing a shiny, dark blue dress with sleeves that showed off her flawless arms, the blue sapphire necklace my dad gave her for their anniversary sparkling under the ballroom lights.

I whipped my head around and looked for my grandmother. My sister and her dolls were gone which meant they were back in the room. I tore away from Red and smacked my mother on the back, startling her into pulling hastily away from Red's dad.

"I want to go back," I demanded.

"Then go back, honey. I'll be there soon."

"Now! I want to go back and you need to come with me."

My mother glanced up at the man. He squeezed her hand just before letting her go. I didn't know what I was feeling, but I knew something had transpired between them. I didn't get it until years later, when I saw my friend Sheila dancing with my boyfriend at a Homecoming Dance. He squeezed her hand as I cut in, and I flashed back to the man in Murrieta squeezing my mom's hand before she took me back to our room. My boyfriend and I broke up a week later.

When I woke up at three in the morning, long after the dance had ended, and my mother wasn't back in the room, I ran into the bathroom and threw up for real. It was the first time I learned everyone has their secrets.

Even parents.

I'll Take Two Latkes with the Christmas Tree

I've always felt religion and politics are at the top of the list of what's wrong with the human disconnection on this planet. Validating this belief are the many times I have witnessed a religious-based family argument. My dad's side of the family was technically Jewish, but they celebrated Christmas and Easter and didn't participate in any of the traditional Jewish holidays. My mom's side of the family was borderline Conservative/ Orthodox Jewish. There were many times the two sides did not mix, especially during the month of December, when the three of us kids were caught in a bizarre crossfire somewhere between potato latkes and Rudolph the Red-Nosed Reindeer.

Organized, human-made religion came to mean nothing to me by the time I was a young adult. Religion has always brought a double standard of discontent within the web of my family. I wouldn't be a bit surprised if my trip into the rabbit hole had a little something to do with the hypocritical upbringing I had in the religion department.

My Lithuanian grandmother Toby made no bones about how she felt walking into a house with a Christmas tree. Grandmother Bess, my dad's mom, made it clear she would not take down her beloved tree for anyone, especially her in-law. During one particular Christmas in the early 1960s, harsh words passed between the adults in the living room where holiday lights twinkled on a conifer divinely smelling of pine. Shortly thereafter, a stoic and angry Grandma Toby was driven hastily back to her apartment by my mother, with me in the backseat.

"I tried, mein kind. I tried. I cannot do it!" My grandmother, her eyes swollen and red, attempted to be silent on the ride back to her apartment, but she soon began ranting and raving in Yiddish, smacking her hand on the dashboard. My mother said nothing as her mother got out of the car and slammed the door.

As we drove off, I turned around and watched my grandmother walk up the stairs to her apartment. She looked a little more hunched over. A little older. "Why was grandma mad about the Christmas tree?"

With a practiced and quick motion, Mom took a cigarette out of her purse and lit it. She inhaled, blowing the smoke out ever so slowly. "Grandma's from the old country. Lithuania."

"Where's that and why is it old?"

"It's where she was born, along with Aunt Dora, Aunt Becky, and Aunt Annie." She took another long hit off her Kent cigarette before continuing. "It's where the rest of our family, her family, was turned over by their neighbors during World War II and murdered because they were Jewish."

That's all my mother said about Lithuania. When I was older, I figured out why my grandmother identified the Christian holiday with the extermination of her parents and siblings in Lithuania, a mainly Catholic country. The theory of epigenetics says we can carry the trauma of our relatives in our DNA. If this is true, the death of my family in Lithuania at the hands of their neighbors may have very well contributed to my meltdown.

Toby never appeared at another Christmas Day celebration at her in-laws'. From then on, every December 25 until we could drive ourselves, my mother would drive the three of us kids the mile and a half to her mom's apartment after we finished opening gifts at Grandma Bess and Grandpa Ernie's house. We would spend an hour with Grandma Toby, listening to her trying to forgive my other grandparents for not being properly Jewish. That grief was bookended by her grief for the family she lost in World War II, the death of her husband from a car crash, and the death of her thirteen-year-old son to a rare cancer. My mother marrying an almost atheist was icing on the cake.

Even as a little girl I felt guilty, and wanted to stay with Grandma Toby since she was going to be all alone on Christmas. No one should be alone at Christmas, not even a Jew from Lithuania. But I had to go back to the Christmas tree and the quasi-Jewish house where my dad, cousins, and paternal grandparents were waiting for us to return so we could continue our holiday festivities, which had nothing to do with the birth of Jesus.

Families of mixed religions have gone back and forth between holidays for centuries, but confusion came early for me because my family is supposedly one religion, Jewish. Traditional Jewish families don't have a Christmas tree or hide Easter eggs in their backyard. We were obviously far from traditional. No one else I knew back in the 1960s and 1970s growing up in the San Fernando Valley shared all their holidays with two separate factions of their families. The plus side of the family celebrating everything was that December meant the month was chock-full of presents. We would celebrate Hanukkah with one side of the family, sometimes at a different house for all eight nights. Then, on Christmas Day, we would be with my dad's side of the family.

In December of 1969 we lived in Reseda, California, long before it was hip to hang holiday lights on your house starting in October. Back then, Christmas lights were pulled out of storage a few days after Thanksgiving, not before Halloween.

Multi-colored bulbs were strung over rain gutters, up trees, and around porch railings on all the neighborhood houses except ours. But that didn't stop my mother from loading up the neighborhood kids in our blue station wagon every year to look at house after house covered in lights somewhere in Woodland Hills. It was called Christmas Tree Lane and still exists today.

If we were true Jews, we wouldn't have wasted gasoline driving up and down Candy Cane Lane, Christmas Tree Lane, and Santa Claus Lane oohing and ahhing at plastic, animated angels singing "Silent Night." But again, the lines of religion were blurred in my household. What was religiously inappropriate never crossed the mind of my mother, who just loved to look at pretty lights. She didn't care if it made her mother angry.

My father was anti a lot of things but mostly he was anti-religion, and no occasion brought forth his true feelings on the subject more than sharing Passover dinner at Judge Wapner's house. It's where we spent most of our early Passover dinners. Grandma Toby's niece had married a man who would later become the first television judge on People's Court. We read from the Passover book, ate *tzimmes* made from sweet potatoes, drank grape juice while the adults sipped Manischewitz wine, and ran around the house trying to find the hidden matzah so we could get the twenty-dollar prize.

Being the first one to find the hidden piece of matzah was my favorite part of Passover dinner. We searched the bookcases, between couch cushions, under the area rugs, and in the refrigerator. And just as the winner was given the money to put in his or her college account, voices from the adult table would begin to rise.

Grown-up conversations inevitably turned to politics or religion. Left versus right, or God versus no God. Judge Joe Wapner and Dr. David Powells, the pharmacist, were on different sides of the political train, and neither of them was adept at holding back how they felt. After a while, my father stopped going to the gatherings at the Wapner house altogether, and another page of my hypocritical religious upbringing was torn out of my book.

Three additional significant turning points helped shape the way I feel about religion. The first occurred about eighteen months before I turned thirteen. I had started my Hebrew studies at a small temple in the middle of the San Fernando Valley, Temple Judea. Most of the adults in my life thought it was important I enter the world of womanhood via the Jewish tradition: by going through the motions and subsequent ceremony called the Bat Mitzvah. This is a rite of passage, a crossover from childhood to adulthood. At that point, the child, who is no longer a child in the eyes of Jewish law, becomes responsible for their own deeds, spiritually and morally. Jewish law holds parents accountable for their children's faults and errors until the day before the children turn thirteen. But at that ripe old age, parents are no longer liable if their little darlings cause damage, steal anything, or lie. I think a Bar or Bat Mitzvah is more a celebration for the parents, even if they aren't the ones studying a language in which you must learn to read from right to left. It's a reason to be joyful for the Bar Mitzvah boy or Bat Mitzvah girl, who are now at the age when personal responsibility dawns. Allegedly, parents are no longer blamed for their child's misconduct, and the child can be proud of the new responsibility. As if any thirteen-year-old is fully responsible for anything.

I never made it to my Bat Mitzvah in 1972. One day I was practicing my commandments and the next I was pulled out of my Hebrew studies, left to carry on my early teen life without the ritual I had been looking forward to for months. Many of my friends were studying for the big day. At school, they gossiped about the party and the presents and carrying on the tradition for their families. I was looking forward to that rite of passage when it was taken away.

The reason I was pulled from my studies came down to money. My dad told my Grandma Toby that if she wanted me to have a Bat Mitzvah so badly, she should be the one to pay for it. She didn't see it the same way. I was his first-born-daughter, so my father was technically responsible for the expense of this religious ritual.

The fight took place over the phone. I can still see Mom pacing in our Encino kitchen, the long, beige telephone cord swinging up and down and smacking against the wall as she gesticulated with her arms, yelling at her mother on the other end of the line. My mother was having a tantrum and when she does, she usually gets her way when there is money involved. This time, however, she did not.

"Ma!" she screamed. "How can you expect her to get Bat Mitzvahed if we don't have the money? David isn't going to pay for this so if you want it so bad, you pay for it!"

Not only did I miss out on being carried around a ballroom high on a chair above my friends while the band-for-hire played Hava Nagila, but I also missed out on opening a bunch of envelopes with money in them. And I didn't get to read right to left from the Torah. I turned thirteen the summer of 1972 and remained the responsibility of my parents.

As it turned out, my rite of passage was expendable. Five years later, my brother read from the Torah, danced until midnight, and opened a bunch of envelopes with money inside, leaving me to wonder: If I had had a penis, would my outcome have been different?

The second time I felt the sting of religion was a year shy of my confirmation at a temple high above the San Fernando Valley and the 405 freeway. I was fifteen. In some Jewish circles, the ritual of confirmation was said to be created by the reformed faction in order to keep the child interested in Jewish studies for as long as possible. I had already lost interest, but because attending confirmation classes was my mother's idea, and one of my girlfriends brought a joint for us to smoke before class, I went along. Pulling me *out* of confirmation classes, however, was once again my father's doing.

There was some misunderstanding about families being asked to donate extra money to the temple because of a swimming pool installation. The misunderstanding led to a heated discussion between my parents and Grandma Toby. Again.

"I am not giving that temple another goddamn cent! Do you hear me? Not—another—cent!"

"David! They don't want the money for the pool, they want it for her confirmation fee."

"Ask your mother. She's the one who wants her to get confirmed. Last I heard you didn't really care!"

"How can you disappoint your oldest daughter? Again!" My mother tried, but her tantrum didn't win this time, either.

Again, I got the short end of the religious stick. My father refused to pay anything extra for my confirmation fees so "that fucking temple on the hill" could build a swimming pool. "They can stick it," said my father before walking into his garage/man-cave, slamming the door behind him. My Jewish studies ended once again because religion had turned into a money issue. It was my first light bulb moment, connecting the line between religion and money and how the two often slept together in the same bed, no matter what the religion.

The final nail in my religious coffin was hammered in during my second year of college. I flew down to Los Angeles from Humboldt State to attend the Bat Mitzvah of a cousin. There were three young ladies being celebrated that day. The synagogue was full of family and friends. I expected the usual introduction of the girls, the reading of the Torah, and all the other ceremonial happenings. What I didn't expect was the Rabbi going into a political rampage about the Middle East, even before the Bat Mitzvah ceremonies had begun. I also didn't expect to be asked to put money in a basket being passed around because Israel needed weapons. It was so out of context and so wrong for politics to be brought into a house of God during a Bat Mitzvah ceremony that

I vowed to lead a life exclusive of any kind of organized religion from that day forward. It made no sense to me that religions touting love and truth could be so hypocritical in the same breath.

In one of his songs, Jimmy Buffet sang something about there being a thin line between Saturday night and Sunday morning. We must have shared similar hypocritically religious childhoods.

In the middle of my crackling mind, perhaps I should have joined some sort of religious something. Maybe a connection with God or Buddha or some other higher power could have saved me from a daily prescription routine. However, it would have been difficult for me to hunt for a savior when it was almost impossible for me to muster enough energy to get out of bed, let alone take a shower or brush my teeth. And in 2001, Google wasn't yet the speedy and instant gratification highway it is nowadays. I would have had to make an effort to find a spiritual awakening, and just the word "effort" itself was exhausting.

There was Nothing French About that Kiss

During my years in the Paramount Pictures music department, once a month I would go to a place in Studio City called The Sportsman's Lodge. It was a well-known resort compound consisting of several acres at the corner of Coldwater Canyon and Ventura Boulevard in the San Fernando Valley. Receptions, conventions, and family gatherings had been held there for decades. I could never figure out why it was called the Sportsmen's Lodge because to my knowledge, no one competed in any type of sports at the facility.

The California Copyright Conference (CCC) met there monthly so various people in the entertainment industry could hobnob, flirt and keep up with the latest music industry copyright information. It was one of the rare moments when music publishers, music attorneys, film and television music executives, and music clearance specialists, like me, were in the same room together networking, and eating questionable food. But before Paramount and the CCC meetings, there was my first ever French kiss at the Lodge.

I attended many Bar and Bat Mitzvahs during my middle school years, and it was at one of those events when thirteen-year-old Danny-something was bumped up into adulthood at some temple in the San Fernando Valley. The evening reception was at The Sportsmen's Lodge.

The year was 1972, the same year I was supposed to have my Bat Mitzvah which never materialized. Instead, I attended everyone else's parties. For Danny's celebration, I wore a long-sleeved, floor-length dress patterned with pink and red flowers. It was also the first time I wore heels, so the night was a bit wobbly to begin with. My dress was clingy and silky, and after the traditional Hora dance where the Bar Mitzvah boy sits atop a chair carried all over the room by relatives, a boy named Arnie took my hand into his sweaty palm and led me out the glass doors into the dark autumn night.

I wish I could remember exactly what he said that made me agree to go outside with him. The fact I let some strange boy lead me outside was astounding. If the grown *me* could have warned the young teenage *me* that night, I would have screamed a resounding, *No! Don't go!*

There were artificial ponds and creeks running throughout the lodge grounds, and we walked up and over a few small, wooden bridges. While standing at the apex of one of those bridges, Arnie let go of my hand, took me by the shoulders, and shoved his tongue into my mouth. Past my braces it went, squirming its way inside like it was trying to find a lost coin between the cushions of a sofa. Just as his hand slipped down and brushed the top of my left breast, his tongue was poked by a piece of metal that had come loose and was sticking out of my braces. The tongue, a torpedo zeroing in on its target, had suddenly changed course. His head snapped back, and he looked at me as if I had jabbed his tongue on purpose with the metal in my mouth.

"Ouch!" he cried. "Whaddya do that for?"

"My braces. I'm sorry. I ..."

And he was gone. Mission accomplished.

Asshole.

What the hell had just happened? He didn't ask permission to invade my mouth. I was out of breath and shocked because he'd kissed me, touched my boob, then bailed after my mouth attacked his tongue. I should have slugged him, but I was a bit traumatized. He left me standing alone on the bridge. A large, gold koi stared up at me from below, its mouth opening and closing, opening and closing. I had a fleeting thought, wondering if my braces attacking his tongue had been the excuse he needed to bail as fast as he did. There were no awkward good-byes, no hand-holding. He just split.

Then, as I took a step off the bridge, the heel of my shoe got caught in the hem of my long dress and I lost my balance. I tumbled forward into the railing that separated the walkway from the koi pond. My left hand grabbed the top of the railing, preventing a nasty fall, but my glasses flew off my face and my long hair got tangled in a bush with red berries.

Once untangled, I brushed myself off and looked at the Bar Mitzvah party through the floor-to-ceiling windows. I saw Arnie in his camel-colored jacket, surrounded by a bunch of smirking boys who kept glancing outside, trying to see beyond the reflection of the large windows as if they could somehow get a glimpse of the teenage girl with big boobs whom he had just nailed.

I did not go back to the party.

Returning inside would have exposed me to a certain humiliation by the silly boys who would have had their tongues wagging, as well as being trailed by the silly girls who would have cornered me to get detailed information on what kind of kisser Arnie was. I called my mother.

"Mom, can you please come get me?"

"Now? It's only nine o'clock and we were just …"

"Mom!"

"Weren't you getting a ride home from Betty's mom?"

I tried not to cry but I wasn't very successful. "Now, mom. Please!"

"Did something happen?" She was suddenly alert. "I'm on my way."

We always remember how people make us feel. I felt embarrassed and confused about that night and wondered if I was the target of a bet I had somehow lost. I know a fragment of my innocence was rubbed away by the Arnie encounter, much like sterling silver that tarnishes, and we try to rub the piece hard to get back its original shine. I was tarnished that night and a piece of my shine disappeared.

The disgusting kiss-and-run was another moment that may have contributed to what happened to me during the eighteen months starting in 2001 when all hell broke loose in my brain.

I was an innocent young teen. How was I to know that some thirteen-year-old boys were scammers and heartbreakers in the making? They were up and coming con artists who practiced their moves on naive and gullible teenage girls.

The Boy Called Wayne

I lost my virginity on Halloween night in 1974 to a boy called Wayne. We were in his bedroom. The room was dark. Music from the album *Destroyer* by the band Kiss was swirling in the background as Wayne unhooked the back of my white Maidenform bra. Peter Criss, the band's drummer, sang "Beth" from a record player that was on the shelf in the corner of Wayne's room. The curtains were drawn, and I'm pretty sure his mother was listening on the other side of the door as I laughed and cried when he finally got it inside of me.

After the big night, I started to notice bizarre things Wayne did that were dismissed by his mother as normal teenage boy stuff. His mother thought everything he did was normal. I didn't know I was supposed to pay attention to seemingly innocent taunts, like the way he pinched his younger sister's butt or other body parts when she walked past him in the hallway. The haunted look in her eyes when he would do something inappropriate right out in the open was a red flag. I didn't recognize her look back then as a probable call for help. To my fifteen-year-old self, it was just the glance of an exasperated tween whose older brother was being a jerk. I thought it was the same look my younger sister gave me when I irritated her over something like playing music too loud or taking up too much time on the family phone.

It literally made me sick when the truth finally came out decades later about what he had been doing to his younger sister behind closed doors during the same time I was his girlfriend. In his mother's eyes, Wayne could do no wrong. She had to have known what he was doing to her twelve-year-old daughter, and it disgusts me to think she let him abuse his half-sister right under their roof.

Wayne and I had met that summer over a demolished mailbox. It was the summer before my first year in high school, back when high school started in the tenth grade.

Our younger sisters were best friends in middle school. I went with my mother to drive my sister over to their house, and there was Wayne fixing the mailbox that had been blown up by some neighborhood kids the night before.

He was in a foul mood. I went into the house with my mother, met his and Tammy's mother, then drove back home, leaving my sister at their house.

When we went out on our first date a week later, he drove up in his blue Datsun 280Z. By the time the school year started in the fall, we were a couple.

Not only was my boyfriend a senior, but he was also a star basketball player for the high school team. I was the girlfriend of one of the most popular boys in school. How lucky could a girl get?

He was always looking in a mirror, sticking out his tongue, mimicking Gene Simmons and making sure his straight, black hair was in perfect order. There was a full-length, ornate mirror in their hallway, and it was his favorite place to stand and flex his muscles. He would nod at his reflection and make some absurd comment about going out with himself if he could. His obsession with Kiss was impressive, but at the top of the list was the fascination Wayne had with himself. He was neurotic about how he looked, fueled by the pedestal his mother had been putting him on since he was a young boy.

He had a twisted and distorted relationship with his mother, who treated him like he was a prince. Wayne could do no wrong. He was the product of his mother's first marriage, didn't have to work for anything, and walked around school and his house as if he were God's gift to humanity. His mother was constantly taking his side if we were engaged in a spat and was always putting herself in the middle of our disagreements. Within months, cracks started to appear in my first relationship.

We liked to go to Carl's Jr. in Sherman Oaks for burgers. Wayne called me a cheap date, which worked for him because he never held a job while he was in high school. One afternoon we took the food to go and on our way up Hayvenhurst Avenue, we threw the paper bags filled with empty burger wrappings and french fry containers out the window. A car behind us honked. Wayne thought it was funny.

"Turn around. We shouldn't have done that," I said.

"Fuck no."

"There is trash all over the road. Our trash! We have to go and—"

He downshifted and sped away from the scene of our crime. "Just shut up and let me keep driving."

"Take me home. Now," I spat.

"Quit being such a pain in my ass," he retorted. The fight continued until we pulled up in front of my house, where I got out of the car and didn't turn around. His tires burned rubber as he disappeared down the hill.

I hoped the driver of the car behind us had taken down the license plate number to report us. I would have immediately confessed my remorse. Wayne would have probably found a way for his mother to cover up for him and get him out of the mess. I still feel guilty about not doing more to make him turn around and get the trash. I should have gotten out of the car at the stop sign and walked back to where the white Carl's Jr. bags were strewn about all over the road.

I should have. But I didn't.

We broke up for a few weeks and he started going out with one of my friends. She and I were no longer friends after that for a very long time. When he finished with her, he came back to me, telling me things about my friend I did not need to know. I let him back into my life, like the guileless teenager I was, believing his apologetic lies. Fifteen is such a difficult age.

Two days after he graduated from high school, Wayne came over to the house and told me he was breaking up with me for good. He had met a girl over spring break at a place called Highland Springs, and had been seeing her behind my back for months.

My first real broken heart. I sat on the curb in front of our home and cried. My friend, Nina, came over to sit with me; we were still talking then.

Teenagers.

I wish it was a phase humans could skip.

My sister and Wayne's sister remained friends, and over the years I've heard stories about him. The breakup was a blessing in disguise. He was a rich loser. Someone who was given whatever he wanted, never worked after school, and was born with a silver spoon sticking out of his ass.

I heard he eventually married. Moved to the Midwest. Had a few kids. Divorced her. Remarried her. Did odd jobs. Worked in security. After his mother died, he allegedly tried to scam his younger sister out of her half of the estate. Figures.

In the 1970s he got away with doing things that would not happen today. I'm ashamed I lost my virginity to him. But what did I know at fifteen?

Not as much as I know now. Man, oh man, to have the brain of a sixty-year-old in a fifteen-year-old body!

I didn't find out what he was doing to his sister until years after my infamous broken brain event, but maybe on a cellular level I must have known, and did the one thing I was taught to do by my parents when something serious was going on: Ignore. Ignore. Ignore.

Being with Wayne had many moments of stress and insecurities, especially when he would say things specifically designed to take me down a notch.

"You know you're lucky to have me," he'd declare. "So many girls at school would die to be in your shoes."

Or ...

"Rosanna asked me if we were still a couple. You know Rosanna, the cheerleader with the most gorgeous pair of ..."

Or ...

"The guys on the basketball team asked why I still go out with you. What do you think I told them?"

He was a piece of my peculiar puzzle.

I'm just happy I lost *that* puzzle piece early on.

Golden Arches and Popcorn

I'm sure my love affair with french fries was one of the reasons I thought working at McDonald's was a good fit, so it was a surprise when I was fired because I didn't pack the french fries into those little white paper pockets fast enough.

The hot summer day after I turned sixteen, I applied for a job at McDonald's in Encino, a suburb of Los Angeles split in half by Ventura Boulevard and bookended by the towns of Sherman Oaks, Van Nuys, and Tarzana. By the time I was eight, I had been working at my father's pharmacy a few Saturdays a month. It's where he taught me to count back change so if the cash register broke, I'd be okay.

The cash register at the Schreiner's Pharmacy was an antique. A bell rang on the register and the amount was stored on a large dial in the front of the machine. I still had to add up the products on a separate piece of paper. I can't remember how my dad kept track of the purchases of the day, but it wasn't digitally. My dad held out, shunning new technology as long as he could. I don't think he got a computer in his pharmacy until the late 1980s when the FDA made it mandatory.

Now that I had my driver's license, I wanted a job closer to home so I wouldn't have to sit in traffic on the 405 to get to work.

The Encino McDonald's franchise was owned by the father of a friend of mine. She put in a good word for me and said it would be a cinch to get hired.

I applied for the job, got hired, and was immediately led to the back of the restaurant to a small, windowless office. I sat down in front of a television and watched video after video on how to flip burgers, be nice to customers, fill soda cups, clean floors, keep my hair out of the food, and finally, how to make french fries. The McD's manager in charge was a tall, lanky teen not much older than I. He wore a pink, short-sleeved shirt and a tie with ketchup and oil stains. On top of his head was a red and white paper hat most McDonald's employees wore in the 1970s.

He was very serious about his managerial job. I strove to be the perfect employee. After I watched a few videos, he handed me a clipboard with a test attached. I took the test, did not complain, learned the cash register, and made sure my long hair was properly bound behind my head so a strand wouldn't end up in someone's Big Mac, chocolate shake, or Fish Filet sandwich.

I was ordered to watch the french fry video a few more times because, after a few days, I still hadn't gotten the hang of the one-handed way the fries were supposed to be swept up by the metallic whatchamacallit scooper-thingy so they could slide easily into the white french fry paper pouch. I was reprimanded for putting too many fries into the sack and for over-salting those fake and repurposed potatoes which, by the way, get hard and waxy after an hour.

On a side note, there was even a complaint in 2017 from McDonald's workers (as quoted on grubstreet.com) stating they were made to underfill their french fry orders. Forty years later, McD's is still being accused of scrimping on the fries they sell their customers. Someone even said they were taught how to pinch the fry cartons just right while putting the fries into them, so it looked like the carton or pouch was fuller than it actually was.

The most difficult part of the job for me was not grabbing a hot french fry when it came out of the oil and stuffing it into my mouth.

I may have done that. I may have not been able to help myself.

That may have been the reason I was fired.

French fries were my demise. And maybe one other thing. My job at McDonald's lasted a mere two weeks. For an entire seventy-two hours, I let myself dwell over the fact that if I couldn't make it at McDonald's, who else would have me? I called my friend, Lori, to lament.

"You're not going to believe this. I was fired from McDonald's."

"No way! What happened?"

"I dunno. I think it was the french fries. I couldn't get it right."

"No one gets fired from that place. It must have been something else."

"Well, that geeky manager asked me out. I told him when hell freezes over."

"That'll do it every time."

I couldn't go back to the Beverly Hills pharmacy because my brother and sister had stepped in to help out our father.

I applied to Bullocks Department Store in Sherman Oaks, but I didn't dress the part. I've always been a jeans, T-shirt, and hippie-style kind of girl. Nylons and heels were for other people like my sister, who had fashion style. I was perfectly content in a pair of Levi's, Birkenstocks, peasant blouses, and cotton bohemian clothes with colored fringe and beads sewn onto the sleeves. And I refused to wear makeup. I thought my foundation-free face would be an asset, showing women that they were beautiful just the way they were.

I wasn't down and out for long because working hard had been drilled into my head by my father for years.

He was always at work.

He spent more time at work than he did at home.

I was hired at the Encino Theater, along with my friend Lori, shortly after my brief stint at McDonald's and my failed attempt at retail. I was much better at putting popcorn into a popcorn box than I was at slipping french fries into a paper-thin pouch.

The manager of the Encino Theater was a beautiful, long-legged brunette with wavy, light brown hair just past her shoulders. She wore tailored suits. Soon after *One Flew Over the Cuckoo's Nest* was released, Jack Nicholson came to the theater and sat in the back row, gauging audience reaction to his movie. Of course, everyone loved that movie. It's still one of my favorites.

I was stationed behind the candy counter handing out Junior Mints, M&M's, and popcorn to the theatergoers and wasn't permitted into the theater to watch Jack Nicholson watch his movie. I tried and was told under no uncertain terms was I allowed to leave popcorn duty.

As the credits started to roll, Nicholson and the manager came out of the theater and locked themselves in her office for about forty-five minutes. I doubt he was asking her to critique his film. He left her office first. She came out a few minutes later, her perfectly coiffed hair a little less coiffed. I remember this because she was red-cheeked and wouldn't look us in the eyes as she told us to close for the night.

"Do you think … ?" I whispered to my co-worker as I turned off the popcorn machine.

"Oh yeah. They did it in there for sure. She rarely leaves before we close up," said Barry, who'd been working at the theater for a few years. "Last time she left early was back in February, when Warren Beatty showed up to see how the audience liked *Shampoo*. She's a full-service manager when the stars come in."

I kept the theater job until I left for college in the fall of 1977. Encino Theater was also where I met some rock 'n' roll dude with long, blond hair who took me to the sand dunes of a beach, where we planned our escape from Los Angeles. With help from a bottle of tequila and a joint, I let his condom-covered and very drunk penis thrust sand into my va-ya-ya over and over again. It really hurt. After that I lost interest in seeing him ever again.

At the Encino Theater, I also came face-to-face with my horseback riding trainers from Foxfield Riding School in Westlake Village, Nancy and Joanne. I had ridden English at Foxfield for over ten years, and decided to stop when I got accepted to Humboldt State University.

They asked me why, after all that time and money my parents had spent on my horseback riding life, did I just up and quit? I told them I was leaving for a new life behind the Redwood Curtain and would probably try and ride up there. I never did. I remember the two of them, those twin ladies who had been such a big part of my life, shaking their heads at the same time, sad that one of their own riders with such promise chose college instead of jumping over fences for a living.

I still feel their disappointment to this day. Being a good rider couldn't compare with the lure of getting out on my own and away from Los Angeles. Additionally, owning a horse and competing in the hunter-jumper category was very expensive. It was made very clear to me by my parents that if I wanted to continue competing, I would be on my own financially. I chose college over horses.

Just goes to show we are all only one decision away from a completely different life.

Ten years later, I had my own run-in with Jack Nicholson sometime in the mid-1980s while working on the Paramount Pictures movie lot. I was coming around the corner holding my lunch from the commissary just as he was coming around the same corner from a different direction. We literally ran into one another, my lunch spilling all over the ground. "Pardon me," Mr. Nicholson said, flashing that sheepish and dangerous grin of his at me, and kept on going. The last I saw of him was his backside as it disappeared into the commissary, no doubt on its way to make some million-dollar deal since *Terms of Endearment* had been such a hit.

He did not offer to pay for my ruined lunch. I scraped up what I could and trashed all of it. Had I been as brazen then as I am now, I would have walked up to him and asked him politely to please pay for another lunch.

To this day, I still love french fries, but as good as they taste going in, the process by which my body digests fried foods isn't what it used to be. Once in a blue moon, I will order some fries from McD's, but I order them extra hot. Even then I must eat them fast because they still turn into a waxy un-potato weirdness, which my connection in the potato industry hasn't been able to explain. The only thing he told me was that McD's fries are uncoated. It was all he could say because they have a secret proprietary recipe.

I don't even eat popcorn very much either. Some digestive systems were not meant to run at 100 percent for sixty-plus years.

Too bad we can't just chew the foods we love, but can't digest any longer, then spit out said food product into a spittoon and use it as compost.

I bet Jack Nicholson can't eat fried foods anymore, either.

The Un-Cheerleader

Cheerleaders bounce, and they need to bounce without the distraction of their boobs going up, down, and sideways while they're yelling, "Two, four, six, eight, who do we appreciate?" Or "Fumble it, fumble it. F.U.M.B.L.E. it!"

Unfortunately, I was blessed with the Powells' genes when it came to breast size. My breasts had grown to a solid D size cup by the time I was fifteen, and sports bras had yet to be invented.

So, what the fuck was I thinking, trying out for the high school cheerleading squad? As a matter of fact, why did my mother let me try out for cheerleading? Why didn't my friends try to talk me out of humiliating myself in front of my peers and a few teachers?

The song I chose to bounce around to for the cheerleader tryouts was "I Get Around" by the Beach Boys. Now, if I was the mother of a teenage daughter and heard her practicing a tryout cheer to that song, I would have marched right in there and screamed something about her reputation. At the least, I would have wrapped said daughter's chest in several ace bandages to flatten her out. But my mother was mostly a hands-off parent. It was by sheer luck, and the slight fear of our father, that the three of us siblings didn't end up in jail or worse.

On tryout day, there were students giggling in the audience as I did my routine while one of the teachers covered her eyes. I was *not* chosen to join the squad.

It didn’t matter that I could do the splits or cartwheel and handspring like the best of them. My body wasn’t cheerleading material. Trying out for a sport I had no business being a part of was humiliating. My eyes roll every time I think about it.

I stuck with volleyball, school politics, and carried on.

Years later, I was talking with one of my friends who’d been a cheerleader at my high school in Van Nuys. The things she told me she was forced to do in order to stay on the team were horrendous. There were constant weigh-ins and exasperating worries about weight gain. I was told that the man who oversaw the cheerleaders was especially brutal to the girls about their eating habits and grooming. To this day, I think my friend has some PTSD from her cheerleading days at Birmingham High School.

I suppose my guides and angels were watching out for me that day, making sure I didn’t make the squad. I’ve always had a problem with weight gain, but what can I say? I love french fries.

The Best Friend Who Wasn't

I was nineteen when I learned the hard way that being best friends with someone doesn't mean you tell them everything about your life. When all was said and done and my friendship with Nina abruptly ended, it left a big fracture. Forty-something years later and I have yet to fully recover. Betrayal, in all forms, does that. It siphons the soul, bleeds the heart, breeds distrust.

It was during my second year of college when the person I had called my best friend since our first day of junior high school became the last person in the world I wanted to see. I wonder why she betrayed me in the way she did, even though I've been told for years that pure and simple jealousy had been her driving force in trying to destroy my life.

I'm certainly no angel. I did my own betraying of someone I loved with all my heart. My betrayal is also part of this story.

In 1971, my family had moved from the town in the San Fernando Valley to the hills near Mulholland Drive. I wasn't going to junior high school with my elementary school friends and I was terrified. I had to meet a whole new crowd, and the reflection I saw looking back at me in the mirror was no help. I had long, brown hair, but my locks were overshadowed by a horrible case of acne, glasses, and a large nose. Pre-teen awkwardness at its peak. If I had a dime for every zit and blackhead the dermatologist squeezed on my face between the ages of twelve and fourteen, I could have saved up for a nice car instead of the hand-me-down Ford Falcon I drove right after I got my license.

Homeroom was the first class of the day that September morning after Labor Day. "Go Away Little Girl" by the Osmonds was number one on the Billboard Top 100, and I would rather have been home memorizing the lyrics to "How Can You Mend a Broken Heart" and "Maggie May" rather than trying to make new friends.

I sat in the last seat down one of the rows because we were all in alphabetical order. Nina's last name also started with a "P." She sat right in front of me. As the noisy class settled in, Nina turned around in her seat and introduced herself. We were inseparable from then on.

Her bubbly personality, bright, braceless smile, and thick Coke bottle glasses were too much to resist. I wore thick glasses as well. All summer long I was so nervous about not knowing anyone in junior high, then promptly received the gift of Nina the very first day.

Her last name ended in "ian," which I later found out meant she came from a deeply cultured Armenian family. She had an older brother and sister, and as the baby of the family, got away with things I never dreamed of doing in a million years.

During the early days of our friendship, her parents wouldn't let her spend the night. Nina told me it had something to do with my family being of the Jewish persuasion. I told my mother why Nina wasn't allowed to stay over. My mother was aghast. In the early 1970s, there were still many closed-minded people who thought Jews had horns, were irresponsible parents, and did unmentionable deeds to other children. Bigotry at its finest.

I wonder what Nina's parents thought would happen to her if they let her spend the night. Did they think we would sell her into slavery? Make her eat matzoh slathered in horseradish? Drink Manischewitz concord grape wine? Have lox and cream cheese with her bagel? Were they worried she'd want to convert and end up asking for presents during the eight days of Hanukkah and then demand Christmas gifts as well?

Her parents did, however, let Nina go to the beach with us and eventually, in the ninth grade, they allowed her to spend the night. We spent countless summer days lying on the sand wearing skimpy swimsuits bought at Bea Dyke's swimwear on Ventura Boulevard, while slathering baby oil all over our yet-to-be sun-damaged skin.

I came across a photo of Nina not too long ago when I was going through boxes of photographs, deciding which to keep and which to toss. In the photo we are at the beach, and Nina is sitting on the sand. I wanted to take a picture of her, but she kept saying no. Finally, she peeked out from under her happy-face towel and I snapped a photo. She was holding the towel up to her face. A corner had slipped down and you could see one of her eyes hiding behind her thick glasses. It was the only picture I had of Nina except for a snapshot taken as she walked down the aisle during our ninth-grade graduation from Portola Junior High School. She wore a flowing, yellow Betsy Johnson gown. Her smile was wide and bright, her deceit well hidden behind the oversized glasses that forever adorned her face.

The first time she drove over to my house in her parents' car was the summer after we graduated junior high. She was going to a high school in Woodland Hills and I would be going to the rival high school in Van Nuys. You were supposed to be sixteen to drive legally but that didn't faze Nina. She took her parents' car when they were out of town and drove eleven miles from Tarzana to Encino. She parked down the street so my parents wouldn't see her behind the wheel of her mom's brown Chevrolet. When she told me how she got to my house, I was floored. She made me promise I wouldn't tell my parents she had driven illegally. I felt a pit at the bottom of my stomach at the thought of being cornered by my mom about Nina's mode of transportation. Thankfully, my mom and Nina's mom didn't make a point of getting to know one another, so there was no chance of my mom asking, "Why didn't Nina's mom come in for a cup of coffee when she dropped her off?"

Nina lied so easily. It was something I didn't understand at fourteen. I've always been a bad liar and ironically, it was the incident during my college years with Nina that made me become hyperconscious of what lying does to people. The event made me realize that no matter how much the truth can hurt, I would try to never lie again. I would never betray again because I learned how hurtful it is to be betrayed.

I knew when Nina decided to follow me up to college in northern California there was a shift in our friendship. When she graduated high school she had no direction. We had several conversations during our senior year regarding her reluctance to go to college. She would always bring up the same argument: her dad did very well in business without a college education, so why should she waste her time choosing to sit in school again?

I, on the other hand, couldn't wait to get out of the San Fernando Valley, and made a beeline to the last college in California before the Oregon border. I was there an entire year before Nina decided to pack her things and, against her parents' wishes, head north. I couldn't help but feel responsible for her. I must have encouraged her to get out of her Southern California rut, but forty-plus years have gone by and it's difficult for me to sum up the gist of our conversations about her leaving the safe haven of her parents' house.

She moved into the H street apartment I shared with two other roommates in Arcata. My days living there are something of a blur, but I do recall a moment when Nina was sitting at the kitchen table, her legs crossed at the knee, her foot tapping incessantly on the back of the chair. She was smoking a cigarette and giving me *the look*. It was a look I would come to realize as the precursor to her trying to undermine something in my life.

Later that day, I was sitting in my room with a good friend. My door was closed. We were smoking a joint and talking about going skydiving. Kerry and I were as close as you can be without sleeping together, and his girlfriend had come over to my house looking for him. I'm guessing Nina thought she would catch Kerry and me in the act, because all of a sudden the door to my bedroom flew open and there was Kerry's girlfriend trailing Nina into my room. I saw the disappointment on Nina's face when she caught us doing nothing but smoking a joint. I left Kerry and his girlfriend in my bedroom and went to the kitchen, asking Nina why she just barged in without knocking. She threw me this bizarre and almost hateful look before getting up and leaving the apartment without saying a word.

Shortly after that episode, she moved into her own place with another roommate. Living together hadn't worked out for us. Maybe if I had followed my mother's advice and not moved in with my best friend we would still be friends today. Perhaps, but not likely.

I've made many choices in my life I'm not proud of. I made one of those stupid choices when I was living with my boyfriend in college. The same boyfriend who eventually got away. I moved in with him shortly after Nina moved out.

Nina ended up meeting and then living with *his* best friend. One day she and I were sitting somewhere having a meal, and out of the blue she began talking about an affair she was having with some other guy around town. I'm sure she told me this in order to get me to cough up some deadly information about myself. I wonder if she really *was* having an affair or if it was another one of her lies. I'll never know. What I do know is that I took the bait.

She was one of my closest friends so I should have been able to trust her, right?

I had been having an affair with Max, a tall, blond coworker, and had lied about it to my boyfriend the day he saw Max and me driving together out of the university. I probably made up some lame excuse. I still feel the guilt from my fraudulent words.

Bear in mind, I'm a bad liar.

I let my guts spill all over Nina's ears, telling her every last detail of my affair with Max. How I would drive up to his house in the mountains behind the university and how we would make love for hours while dubbing the likes of Lynyrd Skynyrd, Jackson Brown, and Joni Mitchell from cassette to cassette. How the fireplace crackled as rain fell from the sky and Max and I made love on the quilts his mother gave him for Christmas. How his girlfriend had no clue that we were having an affair.

Within twenty-four hours I would regret every word of that conversation and feel what betrayal felt like for the first time. Mine and hers. It was a double whammy. Karma at its finest.

What goes around comes around. I betrayed my boyfriend. Nina betrayed me. The same day I spilled my secret to Nina, she went straight to my boyfriend, Danny. He was at work flipping pizzas downtown, but she didn't care. She told him everything I had been doing with Max.

Would I have done things differently had I known what the outcome was going to be? Absolutely. I was young and stupid and my hormones were running amok. In the course of my indiscretion, I not only lost a best friend, but also, eventually, the man in my life who will always be my got-away-guy. Everyone has a "the-one-who-got-away" story. Danny was mine.

I never saw Nina again in our college town after that betrayal, except for the one time I was at a stop sign and she pulled up behind me. I stared at her in my rearview mirror. She looked away. I turned around, giving her my best "why the fuck did you do that to me" stare. I stubbornly sat in my car, refusing to move. It was a power play. Eventually she backed up, slammed on the accelerator and went around my car, flipping me off as she turned down H Street.

I thought I saw her once in the early 1990s sitting in the audience of *The Arsenio Hall Show.* I was backstage setting up for the 5:00 P.M. taping when I decided to open the curtain and look up at the audience. I rarely made an effort to look at the audience as they were streaming in for the show. It was strange that all of a sudden I had an urge to take a peek.

I scanned the crowd, then stopped at a woman who looked very familiar sitting halfway up in the section closest to backstage. It was Nina. She stared back, then looked away. Stared back, and looked away. I'm sure it was her. She still wore the big glasses and had the same nervous habit of twirling the ends of her hair. I wanted to confront her, but in the end I said nothing. Even though I was curious as to what her motivation had been for doing what she did to me back in 1979, there was nothing else to say. Her betrayal still stung. It was a reminder of the betrayal I had once perpetuated.

I ruminate over that betrayal from time to time, hers, and mine. It must still resonate somewhere underneath all the other misgivings I've created for myself over the years. Those disloyalties of mine have been thrown into the basket of betrayals I've hidden in the back of my cerebral closet, needing to be set free one day so that I wouldn't drown in regrets. They were stashed behind my basket of duplicity.

Behind my boxes of shame.

Eventually those boxes and baskets spilled out of my mental closet and when they did, I needed help cleaning up the mess. I needed antidepressant drugs to do their thing inside my brain and I needed help from someone who had a PhD in psychology and psychiatry. But what I needed help with the most was forgiveness. Mine and hers. And his.

It's easy to see my part in the betrayal and all the hurt that went around. But it doesn't make it any less painful. Looking back can be either a blessing or just a smothering reminder of what should never have happened in the first place.

The entire incident was a huge soul lesson for me, and certainly contributed to my final break. The betrayals that went around sliced me open and produced a wound that has stuck with me for decades. It's an open wound, and like all open wounds, it has festered, infecting me with the bitterness of my untruths.

Professing for the Professor

I will repeat: I've always been a bad liar. Unlike my childhood friend Nina, who could let lies roll off her tongue as easily as water pours out of a glass pitcher, it never occurred to me to let lying become pathological. The guilt and subsequent pit in the bottom of my stomach that always followed an untruth were much too overwhelming for me to carry around. Telling the truth, no matter what, is the way to go.

Don't get me wrong—I told some whoppers in my younger days, and from what I remember, I think I apologized to those few people I wronged through a lie. But one lie, in particular, stands out. I don't even remember if I ever said, "I'm sorry," to my father, since he was the one who ultimately had to bail me out because of my initial falsehood.

It wasn't just the lie, but the karma that followed me almost instantaneously which had me believing once and for all that what goes around really does come around.

The event reminded me of a scene from the 1981 film, *Clash of the Titans*, in which Harry Hamlin plays Perseus, while his mythological family—Zeus, Hera, Thetis, Aphrodite, Poseidon, and Athena—are up in the heavens determining what situations they can put him in so he will learn his lessons. I'm confident my guides and angels were doing the same to me so I would learn *my* lesson.

It was my first year away at college, attending the school located behind the Redwood Curtain in Northern California. The first quarter was rough. I attributed my two Cs, two Ds and one F to being away from home for the first time, and promised myself I would do better the second quarter. One of my classes was a communications course taught by a gentleman whom I will call Craig. Craig was tall, vibrant, charismatic, and old enough to be my father. He was also engaged to be married to one of the other professors at the university, but I didn't know it at the time.

A month into the course, I had an assignment and was supposed to speak in front of the class. After my speech, I looked over at Craig. He held my gaze for a long time after telling me what a great job I did. Just before the second quarter ended, we were on our way to Lake Tahoe for a long ski weekend.

I told my parents I was going away with some girlfriends.

This was the initial lie.

Technically, I was still a teenager. They say college is a place and a time when people experience all sorts of new and different situations. This was indeed a new and different situation. It was my first affair and only one of the two affairs I ever had with someone who was quite a bit older.

What happened next is how karma played an instant role in my life.

We were driving east along Highway 50, going up the grade just out of Placerville in my 1976 brown Mustang, following a line of slow-moving cars headed to the mountains for a weekend of skiing. There was also an equal number of vehicles coming down from Tahoe on the other side of the road heading west. It was late at night and snowing lightly. I was behind the wheel, and we were coming around the bend near a place called Echo Summit. All of a sudden a white VW Bug from the westbound lane swerved out of control and hit my Mustang head on. If it wasn't for the snowbank on the right side of the road, my car would have plunged over the side and into the South Fork of the American River.

The girl who rammed into me was drunk, and out of the long line of cars going up to Tahoe for the weekend, mine was the one she hit. The phone call I had to make to my parents that night was difficult and embarrassing. Not only did they find out I'd lied about whom I was with, but my dad had to fly up and see that his daughter had gotten into a nasty car accident with a man close to his age.

It must have been terrible for my dad when he found out about the accident. We were not hurt physically, but the disappointment I saw on his face brought me to my knees. I wonder what he was thinking when he realized his daughter was banging her college professor. He didn't scream at me or ground me or tell me he was disappointed. I just knew. It was the all-too-familiar-father-look of his that said a thousand silent words without uttering a single sound. He glared at my lover. For a communications teacher, Craig was rendered speechless. My dad's look had a way of making people dumbstruck.

My Tahoe car wreck caused my parents loads of anxiety. The guilt I carried because of their stress simmered inside me for a long time. If there is even the least bit of truth to the fact that our loved ones who have passed on can still hear us, then I want to say, "I'm sorry, Dad. I fucked up that snowy night in 1978."

Karma had its way with Craig as well. I found out years later that he was eventually fired from the University for sleeping with too many of his students. He married his fiancée but ultimately, she had had enough. Word through the alumni chain is she finally filed for divorce.

My friend and roommate, Paula, who was much more worldly when dealing with men than I was, told me I was an idiot to get involved with a professor.

"Learn from me," she said one night as we were smoking a joint. "Never, and I mean *never* get involved with a teacher or professor. I can guarantee you that their dicks have been in more holes than a golf ball at a PGA tournament."

Did I sleep with any other professors after that incident?

Yes. But only one.

I made sure he wasn't in a relationship and didn't like to ski.

Me Bad Friend

During the spring and summer of 1981, a girlfriend and I decided to take time away from college and travel to Europe.

After we spent time in the U.K. visiting her brother, our Eurail pass took us to Belgium, France, Italy, Germany, Austria, Switzerland, and Greece. We traveled well together, and when one or both of us wanted to split off to explore other destinations, we would make plans to meet up a few days later.

Because our European adventure worked out splendidly, we decided to travel again. We made a plan to drive across the United States the summer of 1982, right after we both graduated from Humboldt State University. I purchased a camper shell for my white Chevy Luv Truck, and we began planning the route which would take us from San Diego to New York and back again.

Approximately a month before our slated departure, my theater arts professor (MTAP) asked me if he and one of his exchange students could tag along.

"I'll have to ask her first," I said.

"Tell her that I'll pay for most of the gas all the way to New York."

I should have said no right away, but this professor could be mighty persuasive and I was a silly twenty-one-year-old with a crush on said professor. Insert eye-rolling emoji here.

Kristen agreed to "give them a ride" to New York so exchange student, Tom, could see the United States before flying back to

Europe. The clincher was the amount of money we would be saving on gasoline.

This was a situation in which putting "chicks before dicks" would have been an excellent idea. Instead, I let my hormone-riddled brain be the driving force in my decision, somehow persuading Kristen it was going to be fun for all of us.

Kristen and MTAP did not get along. He was very intense and often said what was on his mind, sometimes bordering on rude and insulting. But I didn't let that stop me. I couldn't wait to get into a tent with MTAP. I let the buzzing between my legs supersede a good friendship. The look on Kristen's face by the time we arrived at the Barringer Meteor Crater just outside of Flagstaff, Arizona, said it all. I knew I had made a big mistake but I didn't care. We should have driven the men back to Flagstaff and dropped them off. Instead, we carried on like nothing was wrong.

Kristen and MTAP had an argument about something and I was in the middle, trying to placate both of them. The crux of the argument is hazy, but I do remember the look on her face as clear as the day was bright—pure anger at me and the situation. She decided to stay in the truck and not visit the crater. That's how mad she was.

Because I had brought in male energy, our road trip became more about balancing four personalities than about a memorable cross-country adventure between friends. The trip was memorable all right, but not in the way I had hoped.

We made it through the hot and humid south and up the east coast. By the time we got to New York, Kristen was done. I was drooling over my professor while she was made to feel like a third wheel. She did not want to be alone with the exchange student, and I did nothing to preserve whatever part of our friendship was left after this travel disaster.

When we got to New York, she flew back to San Diego, angry at me for putting her into an uncomfortable situation. Even though we had both agreed to bring the men along in the beginning, I don't blame her for how it turned out. When I dropped her off at the airport, she didn't even turn around to wave goodbye.

Kristen never spoke to me again after that trip. I can only imagine what she told our college friends. What I did was terribly selfish.

Years later I found her on Facebook and sent her a private message, apologizing to her for my behavior back then. She never responded.

All these years, I've known how I made her feel that summer because the image of her angry face has stayed with me. I made her feel unimportant. I made her feel like a travel outcast. I'll always be sorry for my part in how a promising girlfriend adventure ended up being a catastrophe for our friendship.

Lessons learned:

Stick with original plans.

Never bring male energy into a girls' trip.

Penises come and go but girlfriends are forever (AKA Chicks Before Dicks).

If I'm reincarnated again with the same MO, stay away from professors.

Back to the City

I didn't want to move back to Los Angeles after college. I had spent the last several years living behind the Redwood Curtain in Humboldt County, and my Birkenstocks didn't smell right in the San Fernando Valley. *I* didn't smell right in the San Fernando Valley. I'd gone to Humboldt State University for a reason: I couldn't stand the city, and Humboldt was the farthest college away from L.A. but still in California so I didn't have to pay the out-of-state fees. But staying in Arcata didn't seem right either. I had caused drama which caused my fiancé some heartache and thought it best to leave so I could figure out my next step.

Danny and I had met in the fall of 1978. I saw him coming out of the school gym with his shirt off. The sight of him stopped me in my tracks. His glistening body, lit by the morning sun and the backdrop of Redwood trees surrounding the track at the HSU Lumberjack Stadium, made for a picture of human perfection. He was engaged to be married to someone attending Cal Poly Pomona but by the following spring he had broken up with his southern California fiancé to be with me.

We were together for almost three years. After the betrayal fiasco where my ex-friend told him of my indiscretion, he forgave me. We became engaged to be married. My mother and I picked out the dress and paid deposits for a stellar wedding at the Calabasas Inn. The date was set for the fall of 1981. We would have been married during our last year of college.

I took off the spring quarter of 1981 and traveled through Europe with my friend, Kristen. It was my last "hurrah" before the wedding. Danny dated a few women back home in Arcata while I was in Europe flinging my way across Greece, France, and Germany. By the time it was ready for me to come home I knew one thing: I was not ready to be married. There was no way I would be able to be monogamous.

A week after I returned from Europe, Danny came over to my parents' home in Encino. He was wearing his torn surfer blue jeans and a white t-shirt.

"I'm not ready to be married," I said. "I'm sorry. I just can't promise to be faithful."

A breeze came down the Santa Monica Mountains, shuffling strands of his straight, golden brown hair, covering his eyes. He stared down at his feet for so long that I wasn't sure he had heard me. He finally stood up, gave me a look that could have withered one of the succulent plants in my parent's backyard, and walked around the side of the house to the front yard. I heard the door to his blue Datsun slam shut, then drive down the hill, away from me and the two people who were supposed to be his in-laws before the year was over. I felt horrible but it was the right thing to do. Danny was an amazing human and I would have made his life miserable.

I heard my parents fighting that night about the deposit money they were losing because I had called off the wedding. I was lying on my bed, listening to their voices rise and fall behind their bedroom door. I turned on my left side and faced the wall, questioning my decision to not marry Danny. Part of me wanted to call him up and say, "Oops! Sorry. Let's get married." But the authentic part of me knew who I truly was and being a one-man-woman wasn't part of my picture in 1981.

The fact is, Danny didn't wait very long to fall into the arms of another woman after I broke up with him. Within a few months, he was with Mary, the woman he'd dated briefly when I was in Europe.

Having fallen for him while I was away, she was right there waiting when I broke it off. Who could blame her? He was a catch, but a catch I wasn't ready to reel in after I returned for my last year of college. Turns out, I was more of a "player" than a "mater."

After graduating the following spring and returning from my cross-country adventure, I moved back into my parents' home in Los Angeles with the intention of saving up enough money so I could go back to Europe and work at a ski resort in Austria. I had the visa paperwork started and saw myself traveling the world. My brother, Robert, even got me a license plate frame that said, "Follow Me and See the World." As the story went, life had other plans.

I lasted at my parents' home for two weeks. After living on my own for over five years, it was difficult moving home again. I ended up renting a room from a writer named Roderick Thorp high above L.A. in the hills of Laurel Canyon. If I had to be in Los Angeles, Laurel Canyon was as good a place as any to hang out. I fell into canyon living, partied with celebrities, did stupid drugs, and forgot about my desire to travel.

Roderick was the author of *The Detective*, which was adapted into a movie starring Frank Sinatra in 1968. He also wrote *Nothing Lasts Forever*, which became the basis for the movie *Die Hard,* but when I met him in 1982, he was down on his luck and about to foreclose on his house in the hills. Having roommates gave him spending money for his alcohol, cigarettes, and pot. *Die Hard* came out in 1988 and turned Rod's life around again. Unfortunately, his unhealthy habits got the best of him and he died on April 28, 1999.

Eventually I landed a gig working in the music department at Paramount Pictures. A far cry from the Pacific Northwest and Europe.

As a kid, I had driven by the movie studio hundreds of times, but never thought I'd be working behind the wrought iron gates where *Star Trek*, *Terms of Endearment*, and *Flashdance* were all produced. My dream of traveling and working in Europe faded with every new show thrown across my desk, and as I got caught up in the glitter of the entertainment business, I forgot about the other life I had planned for myself, which did not include living back in the City of the Fallen Angels.

It was a mistake to let my dream of traveling the world evaporate and waste away because eventually, I was the one who wasted away, smothered under the city I loathed.

Just before I started working at Paramount, I met the man who would eventually become my first husband.

And that, as they say, was that.

My Blind Date with Larry David

I was never into blind dates, but sometime during the winter of 1983 I was talked into going on a blind date with a guy called Larry David. "LD" for short. My friend Belinda knew LD back when they were both living in New York.

Since moving out of my parents' house in Encino and into a rented bedroom atop Grand View Drive in Laurel Canyon, I had rent to pay. Before landing at Paramount Pictures, I signed with a job placement agency and landed a gig with Neil Levin and Company, a hot-shot business management firm that made sure the incomes of Queen, Devo, and Bernie Taupin were invested wisely. It was in the elevator on my way up for my first day on the job where I met Belinda. We got off on the same floor and realized we were both going to work at the same numbers-pushing firm. Kindred spirits, we immediately hit it off. She exuded confidence and had the most engaging eyes, an infectious smile, and the best laugh. In other words, she sparkled.

It didn't take me long to realize accounting wasn't my thing. I worked at the business management firm for two weeks. Belinda stayed at Neil Levin and Company a while longer before moving into the world of talent management.

We remained friends and would scout for guys in the local clubs, hang out with the up-and-coming comics at the Comedy Store or The Improv, and even found out that we once dated the same guy around the same time, a writer named Larry Gross. He thought he was God's gift to the entertainment industry because his film, *48 Hours* starring Eddie Murphy, was doing well at the box office.

Belinda thought setting me up on a blind date was a good idea. I was skeptical.

"Larry who?" I asked.

"Larry David. He's a friend of mine. And he's Jewish. Your Grandmother Toby will love him." Through the phone line I could hear her taking a long drag off a joint, and imagined her blowing it toward the succulent plant in the yellow pot she kept next to her phone.

"You want me to go out with a guy whose last name is the same as my father's first name? A guy who has two first names in his entire name and a guy who is Jewish because you think my grandmother will like him?" I was on a roll. "Belinda, you know I've had bad luck dating Jewish men since my boyfriend back in high school, and on top of that—"

"He's a writer," she interrupted. "You love writers. You want to be a writer. You told me this music business thing you're doing is temporary. A way to pay bills." I heard her unwrap something and pop it into her mouth. The piece of candy clinked against her teeth. "And besides," she continued, "I know he's going to make it big one day. Wouldn't it be great if you got together, and he made it big with his writing so you could quit the music business and concentrate on *your* writing?"

Belinda must have been psychic about how his career would skyrocket because it was *that* Larry David.

The same Larry David who was born near Sheepshead Bay in Brooklyn, New York. The same Larry David who would be *very* involved with the creation of *Seinfeld* and *Curb Your Enthusiasm*.

When Belinda set us up, I did not know anything about him. LD was in between being a writer for ABC's *Fridays* and a writer for *Saturday Night Live*. I agreed to go on a blind date with a then-unknown LD. He called me and I showed up early at our designated meeting place, the Cat & Fiddle Pub in Laurel Canyon.

I was sitting at one of the little round tables in the dimly lit room, sipping on sparkling water when the door to the entrance opened. A tall guy with lots of wild hair filled the frame. Lots and lots of hair. The kind of hair Art Garfunkel had in the 1960s, but way more of it.

He was carrying a script. Not carrying, hugging. The script was clasped to his chest like it was a precious commodity. He didn't let go of his script during the entire blind date. Thinking back, LD was so enamored of whatever the script contained I didn't have a chance. During our small talk, I probably asked him what he was writing. I doubt he would have told me anyway, just in case I might steal his idea. L.A. writers are weird that way.

"If this is going to go beyond a first date and we ever make it to the bed, you're going to have to put that script down. I don't do threesomes," I quipped. He hugged the script tighter.

In a recent interview, I heard him say he hates writing. Why then, on this blind date, was he guarding a script so close to his body? Why did he bring it with him in the first place? Was the script some sort of chaperone? Did a script accompany him on all his dates?

I reached toward the table to grab my glass of water. He flinched and backed away from me, sinking deeper into his chair. Did he believe I was going to grab his script and run out the door screaming, "I have the script!" down the dangerous and curvy two-lane road of Laurel Canyon Boulevard? Maybe it was a New York paranoia thing.

I would have known he was New York born and bred even if my friend hadn't said anything. He had that East Coast grin that wasn't really a grin at all. It was closer to an anxious grimace. It's a familiar lip pose for some East Coasters. The lips are in a straight, tight line, and it almost looks like they'll eventually break into a smile ... except they don't.

And he seemed nervous. Little did I know the neurosis, "bordering on neurotic tendencies" coming from LD that night would serve him well when he created his now-famous television shows.

The blind date was a bust.

Maybe if we had hit it off he wouldn't have been as neurotic as he is. In retrospect, that may not have been a good thing. I'm usually pretty mellow. It takes a lot to rattle my mojo. If we had become an item and my mellowness rubbed off on him, "curbing" his neurosis, *Seinfeld* and *Curb Your Enthusiasm* might never have happened. Both shows thrive on drama and anxiety and neurosis, three characteristics in humans I generally stay clear of.

It never would have worked out with LD anyway. Let's say we made it past the Cat & Fiddle Pub meeting and had a second, third, and even fourth date. By then we might have had sex and I'm guessing our sex life wouldn't have gone very far. I expect certain things from a lover and, well, LD gags a lot. That would have ended that.

I also like to swim and sunbathe in the nude. I don't think he would have dropped his pants without making sure he was in another country where he wouldn't run into anyone he knew.

If he had his famous notepad with him during our brief meeting, I never saw it. He could have whipped it out when I went to the restroom, then shoved it back into his pocket just before I returned to the table.

I wonder what notes he would have made about me? Would he have said I was too much of a hippie for him and that my hair was too long? The cliff notes on Stacey P. would have probably said I wasn't anxious enough or my boobs were too big. I'll never know.

A lot has happened to LD since 1983. I was just a blip in his dating book. I guarantee he would never remember me, the recent college grad with long hair who sat across from him at the Cat & Fiddle Pub when it was located in Laurel Canyon.

I don't know if LD was another one who got away, but he did get away. If it had worked out between us, who knows how that story would have evolved.

On a side note, the story between Belinda and me eventually came to an end. Again, my fault. Some years later, I introduced her to a colleague of mine at Paramount Pictures. Shortly thereafter, I found out he was engaged to be married and I didn't tell her. I didn't know how to tell her because she was falling in love with him. I didn't want to break her heart but I ended up breaking it anyway because she found out, asking me straight up if I knew and why I didn't tell her. I didn't have a good answer. I was a coward.

Disappointing Belinda was cause for a chasm, mine and hers. I adored her and felt we were kindred spirits, but my decision to keep quiet put a crevasse between us. It has never fully healed. Lesson learned: Never cross a Sagittarius.

The Pill Pusher's Daughter

My favorite scene in the movie *Armageddon* starts when the asteroid is about to crash into Earth, but instead, it shatters into a million little pieces as soon as Bruce Willis flips the switch and ignites the nuclear weapon.

No matter how I word it, phrase it, feel it, or hear myself say it out loud, I know this brain of mine wasn't supposed to shatter into the million little pieces it did because I was never permitted to fall apart. If my dad were alive when it finally happened, he would have been more than disappointed.

I was the one who seemingly had it all together… just like him.

I was the one who had direction and stability… just like him.

I wasn't allowed to break down … just like him.

But I did.

And in his own way, so did he.

He didn't fall apart like a tower made of cards crumbling to the ground when a gust of wind blows through an open window. Nor did he have a breakdown which left him catatonic or on antidepressants. He fell away from his family like muddy riverbanks that collapse when turbulent floods erode at their foundations little by little, piece by piece, year after year.

In trying to understand my father after he was already dead, I learned he began to fall away from so many things in his life long before I was born. He used his pharmacy— and the drugs that came along with being a pharmacist—as a way to absolve himself from who he really wanted to be and what he really wanted to do with his life. It was his Beverly Hills escape room. What his heart wanted had nothing to do with catering drugs to the rich and famous in Beverly Hills. His heart wanted a life in the mountains where fishing at sunrise would have been his norm. He's the reason I presently live high in the Sierra Nevada Mountains.

My sister once told me she could speak to the dead, and said our dad was angry that he died before his mother-in-law. She told me he missed scrambled eggs in the morning and jelly-filled pastries from the café across the street from his pharmacy. I told her to ask the next time she talked with him whether he missed being alive, and if he had to do it all over again, would he take care of his prostate cancer while it was still in its early stages, instead of trying to be the first pharmacist on record to attempt curing it homeopathically.

I wanted her to ask him: If he had to do it all over again, would he decide to tell me he had cancer when he first found out about it, or would he have kept it from me for three years until there was no hope for remission?

The cancer eventually destroyed my dad and robbed him of the possibility of a life well lived. Cancer was the excuse he needed to avoid facing the fact that the life he had created for himself wasn't working the way he had wanted. He no longer had to hide his disappointments under an umbrella of drugs and whatever else he did when he wasn't home with his family. He found an easy way out. A slow suicide.

I missed my chance to yell and scream at him and make him feel guilty about keeping that cancer-infested organ inside his body so it could devour him from the inside out. I didn't get to try and make him see that he was important to all of us and that his grandsons needed him.

I needed him.

There must be a phrase or a word that perfectly describes what you go through when you live in the same house with someone and you're too young to realize their unhappiness is growing along with you. Like the growing pains our bones endure during the pre-teen years, the pain of our parents' decisions made before we were even born lie just below our skin. If the sun hits it just right, the outline of that pain is visible to the world. Sometimes we get a notion as to the point of its origin, but then it escapes because it wasn't our pain to begin with. I was born and dumped into the middle of my parents' story, which had time to simmer long before I was conceived.

The phrase I'm thinking of goes something like, "You can't save someone from their misery, but you can save yourself from their misery." Is that what I did? Saved myself from my father's misery instead of trying to understand it? Instead of trying to help him comprehend and move away from whatever was making him miserable, was my unconscious ignorance of his internal desolation the one thing that eventually took me to the point of no return and my breakdown? I watched my father suffocate himself with his own sense of responsibility, and I did nothing to stop it because I was doing the same thing.

Knowing and unknowing my father the way I did, it's easy to see how the half of him who is part of me could be put into my "maybe-this-is-why-I-cracked-up" pile. Like everyone else in the family, I grew up ignoring my father's problems. By the time I could pinpoint the reasons for his unhappiness and dissect the causes, I had allowed myself to be overtaken by the misery of another person: my first husband.

I've tried to study my father's path to find out why he gave up on so many opportunities, letting his world slowly collapse around him. He gave up on the things that brought him joy: going to the swap meet on Sundays, playing handball, visiting his gun club, camping and fishing, his 1952 MGTD. When he sold that green treasure, his beloved car, I knew something was up, but having a serious conversation with my dad about his life wasn't something any of us did. My father never pulled me into a corner and asked how I was doing. Ever. It seemed like he didn't want to talk to me at all.

Similar to the history of my mom's side of the family, the making of my father's history is splintered into several factions, all combining to create the persona of the man who chose cancer as his way of leaving this planet in order to start over. If the theory of reincarnation and other worlds holds true, he can be someone else entirely by now. Perhaps he's on his way to becoming that hermit in the mountains he longed to be while he was still here, begrudgingly connected to us.

The stories I gathered about his life were from other people: his mom, his dad, his sister, my mom, and a friend or two. I would work in his pharmacy when I was in middle school, and an agent or celebrity would come in and I'd overhear them talk about things I was supposed to ignore or pretend I didn't hear or understand. Things that led me to believe his family wasn't his problem, but rather an insignificant part of his life that he treated as a burden.

He was born in Los Angeles, the firstborn to a set of parents who'd started their lives in the upper Midwest. I know he was teased a lot because of his weight, and that my grandmother used to spank him with a fly swatter when he was out of line, or if he was blamed for something that was his sister's fault. He got injured playing football in high school, which was truly unfortunate because football was his passion. Until the day he died, my dad held a deep longing for a beloved sport he was no longer permitted to participate in.

Except on Sundays.

When football was televised only on Sundays, he lost himself in the touchdowns, field goals, and head-on concussions while my mother took us to the beach, Disneyland, or to our Grandma Toby's home near the Farmer's Market in Los Angeles. She needed to get us out of his hair. Sundays were supposed to be his quiet day. He'd tell our mother that he has to deal with people and their problems all week long at the pharmacy, so why can't he have a little peace and quiet in his own home? My question is, why did he allow his customers to zap him of the energy that should have been saved for his family?

My dad's mother, Grandma Bess, told me that his back injury in high school was when his mental fracturing may have started. When he lost the ability to eat, drink, and sleep football, his world stopped. He shut down.

Eventually, he found solace in the U.S. Air Force and was determined to be a lifer, but then he met my mother on one of his leaves. They were set up by my mother's sorority sister, my Aunt Susan. There couldn't have been two more different people on the planet than my parents. He loved sports. She loved shopping. He loved camping and fishing, which she hated. He wanted to move out of Los Angeles and be a pharmacist abroad. She refused to leave her mother alone in L.A..

Even though they had stayed married until he died of cancer at the age of fifty-eight, I'm not so sure it was a match made in heaven. Didn't he think he could find another woman to marry? Was he pressured into marrying my mother by his parents because her mother owned property? Did they really love each other? I'm sure there was love, but were they ever *in* love? And why did he stay engaged to her when he realized it wasn't in her plans to become an Air Force wife? Did he know that *before* they were married, or did she wait until the honeymoon to tell him she would never be the kind of wife who moved from base to base and raised Air Force brats?

When he became engaged to my mother, his parents talked him into doing something practical. Something that would make *them* proud. Maybe that's just who he was, a pleaser, shoving down whatever *he* wanted to do for himself in exchange for a life of settling because it was the right thing to do.

In due course, he left everything he loved about the Air Force, married my mother in a lavish Jewish wedding at some temple on La Brea Boulevard in Los Angeles, and tried at once to become a veterinarian while working two jobs. He loved animals and wanted to be around them. I understand that, because he never came across as someone who loved people very much—which is ironic, since he ended up in the school of pharmacology at USC. As a pharmacist, he was around people and their medical complaints all—day—long.

Should he have kept trying until he made it into veterinary school, or was he under the gun to get a career wrapped up because he had a wife with a baby on the way?

That baby was me. A mistake. An accident. A meeting of sperm and egg that wasn't supposed to happen. In 1958, diaphragms were not 100 percent effective in preventing unwanted pregnancies. I'm living proof.

I ruptured into this world already knowing at a subconscious level that I was another cause for the fracture in the life of my father. I was someone who tied him down when all he wanted was the courage to wander free. I wonder what that moment was like when my mother found out she was pregnant and told my father. They had been married for only three months. Did she wait until the right moment to tell him, or did she make him go with her to the doctor's office so he could be there when they took her blood to confirm I was on the way? Was he sitting under a dull lamplight in a corner of their living room studying chemistry when my mother dropped the news? Did she tell *him* first or her mother? Did she tell *him* first or did she tell her best friends first? Was she happy or scared to make the announcement?

My mother once told me that if abortions had been legal in 1958, I wouldn't have had a nervous breakdown because I would not have been here. I wouldn't be trying to figure out why such a responsible person like myself found solace and discord in such a dark place. Maybe the genetic pattern was already set and I was on the highway to self-splintering during my mother's second trimester. Did my parents have fights like most newlyweds about money, spending time together, not spending enough time together, how to pay for a baby who wasn't planned? It makes me wonder if I felt the anxiety in utero and decided then and there to become the most responsible offspring ever, no matter how much my burden of responsibility would weigh me down way into my thirties and forties.

My dad did what he thought was the right thing to do, and tucked away his dream of tending to animals or moving to the mountains in order to spend his days mixing chemicals, selling toothpaste, and dispensing drugs to the one breed of living species he seemed to loathe: humans.

And he didn't tend to just middle-class folks.

During his tenure at USC, he got a job in a pharmacy working for a man who catered to the crème de la crème of Los Angeles. Theatrical agents, celebrities, and the finest Beverly Hills MDs flocked to the little pharmacy at the heart of movie star land, and my dad was there to cater to their every chemical and neurotic whim.

His responsibilities became twofold when his boss retired and sold him the business. Out of the house by six in the morning and not home until way after the sun went down, he gave his life to the pharmacy. Everything and everyone else who lived with him became his liability. Counting pills was his escape. When he came home to his two-story house in the hills, the "closed-for-the-day" sign went up all around him, shutting out the people who loved him most.

It was a Saturday evening after spending a day with him working behind the cash register when I decided we should have a talk. We were in his yellow Jeep, driving north on the 405 freeway, and like most kids in high school, I felt brave enough to assert my independence by questioning his decisions.

"Why are you still here in Los Angeles? You hate it down here."

For a few seconds, I didn't think he heard me. Then, "The pharmacy is in Los Angeles. Your mom is in L.A. and so are my parents."

"Didn't you and Mom want to own a bed-and-breakfast in the mountains?"

"Yup."

"What happened?" I was on a roll, feeling brave. I was talking to my dad and happy he was actually talking back.

Again, he waited before answering. We got off the freeway at Mulholland Drive and headed west along the winding road. We passed Ronald Reagan's church on the right, and a swanky private school on the left before the view of the San Fernando Valley appeared, lights twinkling, sirens wailing. As he shifted the Jeep into third, our bodies jerked forward, then back against the seats. "You and your sister and brother happened." He must have sensed that I felt like my gut had just been punched because quickly he added, "And I have too much overhead and responsibility with the pharmacy."

That was the last time I asked him why he stayed in Los Angeles, living in a house in the hills when all he really wanted was a cabin in the mountains.

My dad had an unspoken way of letting those around him know when he was closed up for the night. The barricade would go up. It reminded me of the force field alien ships put around themselves in movies like *Independence Day* so no one can get in. He would lose himself in front of the tube watching *All in the Family* or reruns of *The Honeymooners* and then fall asleep. The option of a verbal exchange with his own family was effectively eliminated. Unless, of course, my mother had to tattle on my brother, who always seemed to get into trouble. Sons will do almost anything to get the attention of their fathers, even bad things like blowing up a neighbor's mailbox or putting a hole in a bedroom door with a closed fist.

I hope my brother realizes that our father was somehow broken, and there was nothing any of us could have done to shatter the fortress he had built around himself, systematically keeping all of us out of his private hell.

The pattern of communication with my father had been set long before I ever said my first word, so why was I surprised to find out that my dad had cancer years before I was ever told? I never got a straight answer about who made the decision to keep it from me and why. Did someone say, "Don't tell her you have cancer because …" or, "Better keep this from her because she has enough troubles of her own right now," or, "If we tell her about your cancer then it just might push her over the edge."

Well, guess what? I went over the edge anyway. It was about the time I found out "they" had kept the cancer secret from me for years when my shell gave way to an assortment of fissures. Yes, "they." Apparently, a hodgepodge of friends and relatives knew that the deadly cells were multiplying inside my father, and even though it isn't in my nature to wish ill on anyone, to this day I hope that every single family member of mine who knew about the cancer and made the conscious choice not to tell me feels very, very guilty about their decision to leave me out of the loop until it was too late.

Some things are difficult to forgive.

Maybe if he had told me about his cancer when it was first diagnosed, I wouldn't have found myself years later sitting in the middle of the floor in a newly remodeled master bathroom, surrounded by empty cupboards, sobbing uncontrollably, wondering when things had begun to fall apart. Maybe if he had told me about the cancer from the beginning, I would have been able to forget about my life for a while and help my dad focus on being a cancer survivor instead of a cancer statistic. Maybe if he had told me about his cancer when he was alive and still had four years to live before he finally succumbed to the disease, I would have found it easier to forgive him for choosing that way out. Or maybe, helping him survive cancer would have given me the strength and courage I needed to finally leave my first marriage when I wanted to, not when I actually did.

My Grandma Bess called me the day before her son died, telling me she was praying that he wouldn't die on his father's birthday. He died the morning after, on April 29, 1993, at 6:05 A.M. in the arms of my brother, and me at his feet. His heart finally stopped with the word, "No!" escaping his blue lips.

I wish I knew then what I know now about the afterlife. I would have made his transition easier, calmer. Then possibly his last word wouldn't have been no, but instead, something like, "adios," or, "until we meet again." Up until the last second of his life, I think he was still mad that he died before his mother-in-law, and before he got the chance to escape Los Angeles and move to the mountains he so loved.

He's come to me in a few dreams since his death. One time I was walking around a street in Ireland and saw him waving at me from a pub. I know our granddaughter has seen him. When she was a toddler she used to sit on the floor in our living room and wave at someone only she could see. I had this wall of photos in the sunroom and when I took her there, I asked her who she was waving at. She always pointed to my father. "That's your Great-

Grandpa David," I said, feeling sad that she would never get to know him. She would have been a good reason for him to stick around.

Sometime in 2011, my second (and final) husband and I were at the Bridgeport Inn, a haunted hotel/restaurant along the 395 in the Sierra Nevada. Over my usual meal of tuna melt with fries, I told him about my father and how he had died and how I was still upset about the choices he'd made. My husband left to use the bathroom, and as soon as he was around the corner, my father's voice was in my head, loud and clear, telling me he knew now that it was a mistake to try and use homeopathy to cure his cancer. I shot up in my seat. There was no doubt it was my father's voice. I even looked around to see if he had snuck up behind me. Bridgeport was one of his favorite places to go fishing. Showing up when he did to lament his decision in my ear, although unexpected, was not surprising. Weird things like that had started to happen to me, and around me, but it was the first time I had heard *his* voice so clearly.

In October 2012, I produced a segment of my "Exhausted Parent Network" radio show, and it was all about Halloween. I had a guest caller, Miss Bonnie, a clairvoyant/medium who does phone readings from her home in Ohio. Her schtick for that night was to tell the listeners that, depending on what their astrological sign was, they should dress a certain way. When she finished, she asked me how many people were in the studio. I told her there were five. She then told me that her "guides" said we could each ask her one question. I was the last. I asked her why my dad chose to die the way he did.

"Hold on a minute," she said. "He's here, says he's 'reporting for duty' and is in some sort of armed forces uniform." I told her of course he was, since being in the Air Force had been one of the happiest times in his life. Then she said, "He has something to ask you." I waited for about five seconds while Miss Bonnie listened for my dad's question from wherever he was in the spirit world.

"He wants you to know that God has forgiven him, so why can't you?"

I immediately went to the commercial break because I was crying. He was right. Why couldn't I forgive him? Up until the moment when he had asked me that question, I realized I had been harboring deep-seated anger toward him, shaking my head whenever I thought of him because he was not with us. All he had to do was take the damn prostate out instead of letting it fester inside until the cancer metastasized.

With the help from a lot of guides and therapy, I'm mostly over his decision, and look forward to seeing him again on the other side. But not until I'm done with this life. I still have too much work to do.

Besides, he shows up in my head and dreams now and again.

We're cool. I get it now, some thirty years later, but it really would have been helpful if he had been around when I had my outstanding and inescapable nervous breakdown.

#MeToo, #MeThen

In 1990 I was working as the Music Clearance Coordinator for a spicy new talk show. It was my job to make sure all the music used in the show was properly licensed from the copyright owners or music publishers.

Arsenio Hall had become the darling of the late-night talk show circuit and as his star rose, the characters in his entourage and the worker bees backstage at Stage 29 on the Paramount Pictures lot also rose to the occasion.

One of his managers attended the five-day-a-week tapings Monday through Friday, standing backstage as his client did the “Late Night Thang.” Mr. Manager was in his fifties and used his long comb-over to disguise the fact that no amount of hair was going to cover up the obvious. His wire-rimmed glasses slipped down his nose as he rocked back and forth on his heels, observing the comings and goings of backstage. Producers, grips, camera operators, makeup artists, art directors, stage managers, and the prop master scurried around the manager, who appeared to be unaffected by the nerve-racking minutes before showtime.

I rarely spoke with him backstage because I had a job to do, and just as soon as the show was in the can I made a beeline for the daycare center to pick up my kids. He started asking why I sat backstage with a stopwatch or what it was that I actually did for the show. Small talk. One day he asked me to lunch, where we talked about the music business and our families.

The red flag came a few days later.

A large and gorgeous bouquet of flowers was placed on my desk. My music department colleagues were all in a tither, thinking I must have the best husband ever, but I knew better. My husband had never sent me flowers. Ever.

The card read, "Thank you for the entertaining lunch. Let's do it again soon." I was aghast. He knew I was married and had two boys at the daycare center on the lot. I knew he was married. I racked my brain wondering if I had sent mixed messages to this manager. How was I to know that accepting a lunch invitation would be taken as an opening for something else? Why else would he have sent me flowers that were not the cheap, grocery store variety?

I lied to my colleagues about who was behind the gift and dispersed the stunning bouquet into several small vases, which landed on various desks and window sills in the music department. When I saw the manager backstage that day I pulled him aside.

"You can't do that. Don't send me flowers. Ever."

"Why not?" He seemed amused and nonplussed about my request, looking away from me as he watched some woman walk past him and around the corner into the makeup room.

"I'm married. It's not okay. It was just lunch!"

"Okay." He was rocking back and forth on his heels, his mind elsewhere. I was dismissed. Good.

From then on I tried to ignore him for the hour I was backstage, keeping my answers to his music business questions as short as possible. I couldn't understand why he was so insistent with me. It started to get creepy but he never asked me to lunch again.

About a month later he requested I come into his office for a meeting. Mr. Manager told me he wanted to discuss the music business for two of his most famous clients, Eddie Murphy and Arsenio Hall. They both had songs on the Billboard Hot 100. He told me he needed help figuring out how to get their songs into more television shows and commercials. With those two clients on his management roster, this guy was on top of the world both financially and metaphorically speaking.

I told my supervisor, Ridge Walker, that I was going over there, making a joke that if I wasn't back in thirty minutes he should come looking for me. Ridge eyed me through a haze of smoke and raised his silver eyebrows. He shook his head while putting out the cigarette in his Swarovski crystal ashtray, then uttered, "Be careful."

I exuded confidence as I marched into Mr. Manager's office carrying a notebook, telling his secretary that he was expecting me. I was much thinner back then and rocked in low-heeled black leather pumps, a dark gray pencil skirt, and tangerine blouse—acceptable business attire when meeting a high-powered talent manager. The lunch and flowers were forgotten; having a business meeting about the music of two of Hollywood's favorites could be a good thing for my career.

His assistant barely glanced up as she pressed the intercom button on the phone, letting the manager know I was in the waiting room. I was buzzed into an office reeking of money and importance. Bookshelves were lined with photos of the manager next to celebrities and politicians. The wall to my right was covered in plaques. Tall windows looked out over one of the grassy areas of the movie lot and before I could say hello, the large, wooden office door clicked shut behind me.

He came around his desk so fast that I took a few steps back and was up against the door. His mouth was on me, his wet, cold tongue trying to jab through my teeth. I shoved him as hard as I could. He stepped back, slowly, methodically, pushing his comb-over back into place as he smirked.

I was stunned. *Did I bring this on? Is this my fault?*

"What the fuck? You had no intention of talking to me about music for your clients."

"It was the only way I could get you into my office."

"Open the fucking door. Now." I was seething.

He looked at me for a few seconds, shrugged, then pressed a button on the side of his desk. The door swung open and I escaped.

He didn't show up backstage for several weeks after that, and when he finally did, thankfully he ignored me. I was lucky I was a Paramount employee and not a show production employee or I'm sure I would have been fired. The manager had that much power. I also realize now that I should have gone to Human Resources and reported the arrogant SOB.

Another "I should have."

Shortly after locking me in his office, he began having an affair with a friend of mine who was on the production crew. I know this because she told me. I never confessed to her what the manager did to me. I didn't tell my supervisor, my husband, my therapist, or my best friend. What would have been the point?

Another #MeToo moment during my Paramount days happened shortly after DG was hired to run the Paramount Television Music Department. Even though I was working in television, I was still under the supervision of Ridge Walker. Ridge was the Vice President of Music Clearance for the Motion Picture Division. He had initially hired me to work music clearance at Paramount and gratefully, did not make me work under DG.

After he was hired, DG would take various people to lunch, ostensibly to ask them what their job was in the department. When he got around to asking me to lunch, we went across the street to Raleigh Studios, which had one of the best cafés in Hollywood. After we ordered, he leaned back in his chair. He was wearing a camel-colored corduroy blazer with dark, suede elbow patches.

I'll never forget that blazer. Or his arrogant smirk. He looked at me with his hooded, hyena eyes and asked, "So, do you ever fool around on your husband?"

My eyes darted around the room, wondering if anyone had overheard. "Did you just ask me what I thought you asked me?" I was shocked and leaned away from him.

"Well, do you?" His left arm was draped over the back of his chair and he squinted at me through those lowered eyelids, a lame attempt at trying to be seductive. All it did was make him even more disgusting and pathetic.

I shoved back my chair, walked out of the café, and went straight to Ridge's office, telling him that under no circumstances would I ever work under DG. Ever. Ridge never asked me why but until the day he retired, I had nothing to do with DG and would avoid him whenever possible. Again, *I should have* gone straight to Human Resources.

By the time Ridge retired in 2001, I had been living in Santa Clarita, California for a little over three years. I had moved back to the Los Angeles area from Mammoth Lakes in 1998 so the boys could be closer to their father after the divorce.

I was still working at Paramount and telecommuting like I had been doing from Mammoth Lakes since 1992. I was the first telecommuter at Paramount Pictures, working as the Music Clearance Coordinator for *The Arsenio Hall Show* until it went off the air in 1996. I moved back to Los Angeles after my divorce, just in time for my kids to start a new school. Ridge always found music clearance work for me to do after TAHS was canceled.

Ridge was gone, and when it was decided by Paramount—and by that I mean DG—that I had to start coming into the office every day, I knew my days at Paramount Pictures were numbered.

The main reason I moved my family away from Los Angeles in the first place in 1992 was because my asthma was out of control. I was hospitalized several times, two of those times while pregnant with each of my boys. Living in the mountains had healed my lungs and I was on minimal meds to keep them functioning.

That all changed in the fall of 1998 when I moved to Santa Clarita, with the smog and the pollen and the stress of trying to raise two teenage boys on my own. They were dealing with their own messed up worlds, which included the awful divorce and an almost absentee father. He was still in the area until he eventually escaped to Thailand, leaving me to pick up the pieces.

Did I mention that I sucked as a single mother?

The drive from my home in Santa Clarita to Wilshire Boulevard was at least an hour-and- a-half commute in traffic. By then the television music department had been moved off the Paramount lot. I had no one to keep an eye on my kids after school or take them to school in the mornings because their father refused to help me with his own boys. It didn't take long before I was overwhelmed by the stress of everything.

My asthma kicked in full time and with Ridge Walker gone, so was my safetynet. No matter what the doctors said, DG insisted I abandon my telecommuter position and come into the office every day. I finally made an appointment with Human Resources. DG was there along with several of Paramount's finest suits. I poured out all my meds on the table and told them that not only was my asthma in full swing, but that I had managed to avoided DG all these years because he had made an inappropriate pass at me when he was first hired. His face turned red when I recalled out loud our brief lunch at Raleigh Studios. He didn't even deny it. He just looked down at the floor. In the end it didn't matter to the suits that I had been able to work for several years via phone, fax, and computer. They said if I didn't come into the office they would have to let me go, and let me go they did—only three years before I was fully vested in my retirement.

I was told I had a lawsuit against Paramount because I had set a precedent and could prove that I had been working successfully as a telecommuter for years, but mentally I could not handle any more stress.

It wasn't long after that meeting I found myself melting down, wishing I drank alcohol and wondering how many Benadryl pills I would need to fall asleep and never wake up.

The Anxiety of Marriage Number 1

Kidneys have long been thought to be the organ connected to heavy trauma and emotional turmoil. In the Old Testament, kidneys are seen as the gateway to secret emotional thoughts of the human condition. If any of this is true, then my first marriage, being an extreme and tumultuous Sturm und Drang, could have been one of the reasons my left kidney went haywire and had to be removed on December 18, 2008. Renal cell carcinoma is a slow-growing kidney cancer. My left kidney was removed eleven years after my divorce was final.

I met my first husband at a party, and fifteen months later we eloped to Reno on the same day the Mexican community celebrated the Battle of Puebla in 1862. Cinco de Mayo is often confused with Mexican Independence Day, which is celebrated on September 16, when Mexico won its independence from Spain.

We got tethered at the Hitching Post Wedding Chapel, an in-and-out wedding venue on Highway 395 in Reno, where we were charged a $78.00 ceremony fee. If the minister had called to verify the funds on my Visa, we would have been denied right then and there. Instead, we became husband and wife at nine o'clock in the morning, our husky dog, Peppy, standing in as the witness.

With a line of promising soon-to-be-married couples behind us, the merry ministers said their congratulations after we proclaimed, "I do," then shoved us out the back door into a casino, where we picked up a free bottle of champagne.

I called my parents from a phone booth. My father answered.

"Hi Dad. I'm in Reno." I thought the line had gone dead because there was silence on the other end. "Dad? Are you there?" I heard muffled voices and then my mom came on the line.

"Stacey? Why are you in Reno?" She sounded suspicious.

"We got married." Silence. I thought the call had dropped.

"What? You got married?!" I could almost see her throat close up as she sputtered in disbelief.

She was in shock when I told her we had eloped. I didn't find out until I was finally divorced that her shock was actually trauma. Neither of my parents had liked my first husband and they were not pleased I had married him. They had hoped he was one of my phases.

He was a phase, all right.

A phase that lasted fifteen years.

Four months after we were married, he went out drinking after a concert and broke his leg while messing around at a neighbor's apartment. The compound fracture should have been a simple issue of putting the bone back in the leg, letting the wound heal for a week, casting the leg, and then six weeks later he would be good to continue his acting career and trying to be a decent husband. But fate had other plans.

I don't know if it was his karma or my karma, but the temporary half-cast that the doctor put on his leg ended up burning the back of his leg from the top of his thigh all the way down to his heel. It burned the skin and muscle on his heel down to his bone. Third-degree burns. Being drunk and breaking his leg was his fault, but the burns were the result of mass negligence on the part of nurses, doctors, a hospital, the company that made the casting material, and the plastic pillow manufacturer who made the pillow his leg was resting on as his wound healed. His leg slowly burned down through muscle and bone. I learned that what the casting material did to the back of his leg was because of something called an "exothermic reaction."

It's tough enough being married to an alcoholic/addict. Throw in an unbelievable accident that turned into a nightmare and it was a recipe for disaster and turmoil, misfortune and catastrophe, and mind-boggling stress. Both his and mine.

In between the fourteen or so surgeries he needed over a four-year period to repair the burns with skin grafts, Betadine whirlpools, and lots of morphine, his substance abuse got worse, as did his mood swings.

We got pregnant and had two kids in between those surgeries. For years I was trying to work full time, take care of a disabled husband, and raise two boys. Those years took their toll on everything. I'm sure the cancer in my left kidney was a result of the enormous stress I was under during my first marriage. Cancer cells simmered and multiplied as my stress mounted.

Some people would see this type of rock bottom as a gift and use it wisely. Others, like my ex, saw it as a way to victimize himself. Granted, he was indeed the victim of a careless medical system and reprehensible nursing care, but fifteen years of hearing how everything had been taken away from him, how I would never understand what he had gone through, and how I was an insensitive caretaker, wore me thin.

My divorce was the catalyst to my breakdown, the proverbial "icing on the cake." It closed the door on my fifteen-year "phase," and opened the floodgates to what I can only describe as a cascading, complicated cavern of cerebral chaos that lasted in the neighborhood of eighteen long months.

Part Two

"I jumped into bed with most men who gave me a second look
believing each and every time that he could be The One.
It didn't matter if he drank too much,
had no job, or did drugs that scared me.
I gave him all my love, forgetting to keep some for myself."
–Lisa Lucca, *Ashes to Ink: A Memoir*

Mr. Bay Area

On a lark, I snapped another stitch in my seam by doing something I had not done before and will never do again. I am not and at no time have been a serial dater, yet there I was, lured into a chat room on Yahoo.

I was probably bored.

Maybe curious.

Perhaps a little horny.

It was the wrong thing to do, but I had a what-the-hell-you-only-live-once moment and cast my pair of dice into the World Wide Web. It was the fall of 2000. My divorce had been final for over a year. According to Dr. Laura Schlessinger, a radio talk show host who advised divorced women with children not to date until the kids were out of the house, I should have kept my legs crossed and taken up knitting or the violin. But playing the violin didn't make up for my biological need to breed, even though I could no longer have kids. I had had my tubes tied shortly after Erik was born but the urge to procreate was still there every month. Haunting me with the possibility of fertilization at its peak just before, during and after I ovulated.

I moved back to Santa Clarita from Mammoth Lakes in October 1998. I wasn't ready to jump back into the dating game. In my gut, I knew it. I shouldn't have let myself get distracted from my boys, who were having a hard time with the divorce, with their dad, with school, with me. I should have listened to Dr.

Laura, who said divorced parents should pay attention to the kids, not their hormones. I was selfish.

The result of my search and chatting episodes connected me with a man from the Bay Area. He pulled me up on the back of his white horse, rode me around for a while, and then when I least expected it, threw me off. I landed in an emotional mud puddle so big I still find pieces of the hardened dirt stuck in my hair. One day it was this and then the next day it was that. A brief bipolar love affair.

I had been through enough seminars and therapy to know I had somehow attracted that situation into my life. It was too much to hope that someday I would wake up and say, "Wow…that's it! That's what I did wrong." But I really was clueless and in a mental freefall. I didn't see the pattern I had regarding my relationships with men until it was too late, and my cupboards were full of vials containing Celexa and Wellbutrin and other anti-anxiety meds.

After months of chatting, we finally spoke on the telephone. He had sent me a copy of his driver's license and verified that he really did make a habit of working for start-up companies, then taking their stocks and bowing out. I thought it safe to take him up on his offer to fly up and meet for the first time. Cautious and restrained and slow, I let him in.

On the one hand, I was thrilled Mr. Bay Area could be into a woman like me. I had two teenage boys, a challenging ex-husband, and all the baggage that came along with my dysfunctional, complicated, and tricky life package. He was very good at convincing me that my personal chaos didn't matter.

"I'm going to love your kids like they were my own," he'd say.

"I'm going to buy you a cabin up in the mountains near a lake so you can write all day long," he promised.

"I'm going to take you to Hawaii so you can finally see the lava pour out of the earth."

"As soon as I close this deal I'm going to fly you up here and buy you a safe, new car for you and the kids."

"It will be great racking up all these miles. I can't wait to use them to take you somewhere exotic."

"When my parents come home from their trip, I'm going to fly you up here so you can meet them."

"I think a diamond solitaire would look really great between those beautiful breasts of yours."

And so on, and so on, and so on.

I fell hook, line, and sinker before realizing his charade was one huge stinker.

Should I not have believed him? Was I wrong to trust that he was being authentic and sincere? Did this five-month ordeal contribute to my inevitable cracking, lack of confidence, and ultimate intake of a serotonin cocktail? It did.

I was collecting why-the-fuck-did-I-do-that moments much like Laura Wingfield collected blue roses and glass unicorns in Tennessee Williams's *Glass Menagerie*. I may not have been as physically crippled as Laura, but emotionally, the fissures were starting to display themselves in peculiar ways. The collecting and discarding of Mr. Bay Area was one of my oddities.

The day after he flew down to attend an *Entertainment Tonight* holiday party with me, he called me up and said he couldn't see me anymore.

The conversation went something like this:

Me: "I'm really glad you came down to come with me to the party. I don't think I could have handled the glitter crowd alone."

Him: "I had a really good time. Thanks for inviting me."

Me: "When can we see each other again?"

Him: (Pause … big sigh)

Me: "What's up?"

Him: "I can't see you anymore."

Me: (Long pause…a very long pause)

Him: "I'm sorry."

I was lying on my bed. At this point, I slid down my pillows and tucked myself under the covers.

Him: "Are you there?"

Me: "What do you mean you can't see me anymore?"

I didn't cry or yell or have a drama meltdown. It was the first time, however, I felt the wall climb up and around my heart. I felt it. I could touch it. I thought I could see it: black, sprayed with gray specs of biotite, reflecting, and deflecting, not letting anything or anyone in. At all. Anymore.

Or so I told myself at the moment.

He never explained why he stopped us on a dime. The excuse that finally left his mouth was as lame and insane as they come. He proclaimed the main reason he couldn't see me anymore was because …

Wait for it …

I liked sex too much.

I ... liked ... sex ... too ... much.

Need I say more or does, "You've got to be shitting me?" say it all?

Maybe he didn't have enough money to buy me that diamond, and the only thing he could do was to back out as ungracefully as possible.

I wonder if he learned something from the experience with me. If he didn't, then I hope whoever he ended up with has enough shovels because the bullshit really flowed over the top with Mr. Bay Area.

I was headed into a complete emotional lockdown, an isolation of sorts.

And I had only myself to blame.

I should have listened to my grandmother when she told me boys are trouble.

North Carolina Liar

Michael from high school phoned me out of the blue.

"Michael who?" I asked. There had been a number of boys by that name in my high school, and as I mentally scanned the possibilities, none came to mind. I was surprised and suspicious. Who was this *Michael* calling me?

The beginning of my breakdown was already knocking at my back door, and I wasn't in the mood for a Michael or a Mitch or a Scott or a Greg. Getting out of bed had become a chore, which was bizarre because I'd always been a morning person. The thought of being with someone sexually was unappealing. Also weird because I had always loved sex. How typical of me, back then, automatically jumping to the possibility of sex from someone I may or may not have known from high school. What an awful habit that had become, even though it was waning.

I no longer cared if I colored my hair which, at that point, was about thirty percent salt and pepper underneath the Loreal 7N. I was exhausted all the time and my mood sucked. Then came that call.

"How did you get my number?" I asked. "And you are Michael … who?"

The laugh on the other end of the line was unmistakable. I did know Michael. "Steve gave it to me. He said you guys are still in touch." Steve was Michael's best friend from high school. *Steve and Michael. Best friends. Yes. I know this Michael.*

Last I'd heard, this "Michael" was still married. "Does your wife know you're calling me?" I was being such a bitch and I didn't care. My attitude was another sign that the breakdown had kicked up a notch. I'd been voted "Most Friendliest" in high school; being a bitch wasn't supposed to be in my DNA.

"We are separated and I'm living on the North Carolina coast in my condo," he said, convincing me he wouldn't have called if he wasn't legally separated.

"It wouldn't be the godly thing to do. Call you if I was still married, would it?" He took a breath and carried on. "I'm a church follower and it would be against everything I believe."

My habit was pushing through. Damn it! I didn't try hard enough to shove it away. Maybe this was divine intervention and Michael was the answer to whatever was ailing my pathetic brain.

Note to self: Boys/Men are *NEVER* the answer. Ever.

When he first showed up at my front door after twenty-five years, there was a definite attraction. I couldn't help but feel safe because after all, we had a history. We'd been pals at Birmingham High School, part of the "group" who all went to homecoming together. We were always involved in the same activities, and after football games we would hang out at Dupar's or Pages Restaurant or at someone's house.

When we went off to college, me at HSU and him in Oregon, I rode the bus to visit him up at Eastern Oregon State. That was a weekend I'll never forget. He entered us in a man-made river raft contest sponsored by Miller Beer. As I was floating down the river with Michael, his girlfriend, and some guy I can't remember, our raft crashed into the overpass pylons. People actually cheered as we were thrown off the raft into the freezing water. Wearing a down jacket and hiking boots, I was waterlogged and struggled to swim to the shore. Michael helped his girlfriend to safety and as an afterthought, turned to make sure I was okay and not being carried down river or held under the rapids, drowning.

That should have been my first clue.

It wasn't long after that surprise phone call and our initial reunion years later when the lies started pouring out fast and furious. I bought it all. When someone you've known since you were fifteen years old tells you he moved out of his house and is in the process of getting a divorce, wouldn't you, shouldn't you, believe him?

At first, the passion poured out of us like Kilauea in all her glory, and when he traveled back to tend to his East Coast business, he called every day to let me hear the North Carolina thunderstorms. He wanted to get to know my kids, a sure way to worm his way into my heart. Any single parent knows that if you meet someone and they don't have a problem with the kid-baggage, there has to be hope. His parents remembered me. I remembered them. We had friends in common from the good ol' San Fernando Valley days, and they were thrilled that "after all this time, you guys are finally hooking up." I was ecstatic.

And then …

It's funny how we remember where we were during certain significant events in our lives. I was standing in my parents' Encino Hills kitchen, sneaking a taste of my mother's spaghetti sauce, when I heard Mark David Chapman had shot John Lennon. I was in my parents' kitchen when Elvis had died. When Princess Diana came to her tragic end in a Paris tunnel, I was waiting at a stop light in the mountain town of Mammoth Lakes, California. When my grandfather died, my first close relative to pass over, I got the call when I was breastfeeding my firstborn, and when my firstborn was escorted from my house sixteen years later at four o'clock in the morning to a lockdown boarding school in Montana, I was right there in my living room, in a house twenty minutes from Six Flags Magic Mountain, watching two strangers take the first person I created away from me.

When I found out Michael was indeed still married and had no intention of divorcing his wife, I was relaxing on a lounge chair in my sister's backyard. It was a hot day in Santa Clarita and I drove my kids over to her house for a swim. I was babbling on and on to his best friend, Steve, via my new cell phone, about some music industry issue, when he stopped me dead in my tracks after the conversation turned to our common denominator: Michael.

"What do you mean Michael moved out of his house and into his beach condo?" spilled the best friend. "What do you mean he's getting a divorce?" Steve continued to vomit this new and unwelcoming information until I was covered in a thick ooze of hypocrisy and the walls came tumbling down. The effect of Michael's duplicity was overwhelming. For months he had gone on and on about how connected he was to his church and how committed he was to leading a Christian life. In one moment, it became clear he had been hiding his true self behind that stained glass curtain, and all the Bibles in the world wouldn't be able to save his soul from his hypocritical, fraudulent self.

Michael and I had been great buddies in high school, so I was always under the impression, and subsequent delusion, that someone from my past who might become a part of my present was obligated to be straightforward with me. When I found out he wasn't, that every word leaving his brain and traveling out through his mouth was some sort of wishful thinking bullshit on his part, my personal fracture opened another inch, maybe two. I didn't expect to be the victim of his five-month fantasy. Looking back, I should have seen it coming. *The raft. He didn't save you from the raft.* That's the part of me I'm trying to forgive; the part who didn't recognize the love swindle.. Or, if I'm being totally accountable, the part of me who *chose* not to see things for what they really were. For whom *he* really was.

There are those scenes in movies when someone does something stupid and afterward, bangs her head against the wall because she can't believe she made such a horrendous mistake. That was me. I horribly misjudged the character of someone I'd known since I was a teenager. This incident helped shatter what I thought was my innate ability to judge someone's character. I had no business getting involved with Michael. I was on my verge and his lies were one of the feathers it took to push me over the edge. What he did was cruel, but the joke was on me.

I didn't actually bang my head against anything, but after I took a few deep breaths and made sure my kids couldn't hear me, I called him. Pleasantries eliminated, all bets were off. "What the fuck?"

"Stacey? What's going on?"

"I just got off the phone with Steve. Your best friend from high school? You fucking liar."

"Whoa, whoa. What are you—"

"Fuck off, you motherfucker. You lied to me for months. You are not getting a divorce and you are not separated!"

"Wait! It's not like … I can explain! I—"

"Go fuck yourself." I disconnected the call and my heart at the same time.

As my children splashed in the pool with their cousin I sat there, stunned, letting rage sink into my limbic system, settling there like iced water, solid and expanding, pressing hard against the rocks of its prison until it finally fractured and split, no longer able to contain the frozen force.

I wanted to scream.

I wanted to take the next flight to North Carolina and tell his wife about the last five months. I wanted to tell her how her husband, my dear friend from high school, fucked me on my bathroom counter and on the trampoline in my backyard.

I wanted to sit quietly in the back of his North Carolina church, and when he was in the last five minutes of his "I'm-an-important-man-in-my-church" speech, I'd jump up and tell the pastor and the congregation how this terrible excuse for a pillar of their community, this religious hypocritical man, had promised to fly me out to their sweet little town and let me gaze out over the Atlantic Ocean for days. How he promised me we would do nothing but watch thunderstorms, walk on the beach, and make love between the sand dunes off the cape—just as soon as his divorce was final. The divorce that never was.

I did none of it.

I felt the vortex of my emotions suck down into the zone of unforgiveness, and just like I was taught as a little girl, I pushed them down further. I pushed them down hard and fast and then I told the kids to get out of the pool because we were going home.

For that day, their mom was on overload.

Their mom was done.

Until the next time, that is.

Meatloaf vs. Semen

When I was on the verge of a complete breakdown, occasional moments of clarity sprang up out of nowhere, deceiving me into thinking I was back to normal. There were just enough of those precious moments to make me believe, at least for a little while, that I wasn't going totally insane. Those few days when I woke up and said, "I'm fine and today is going to be a good day," were flashes I would hold on to and hug tight, while praying my dark side had finally grown tired of me and gone on to disturb someone else.

When the journey of trying to convince myself I would never fall apart kicked into high gear, I made spontaneous trips up to the Sierra Nevada to visit friends. The Eastern Sierra sojourn I made that spring of 2001 was my last until I finally moved back to the mountains in the summer of 2004.

I was in a mental frenzy.

It was a mistake to think that removing myself from my environment in Southern California every once in a while would *fix* me back to normal. I had to get away from everything and everyone. I needed space from my kids who thrived off my anxiety, although I would never have told them their mother was an internal basket case. They were exhibiting signs of teens who didn't understand why Mom was crying all the time, and were starting to get away with things normal parents would have noticed. I just pretended not to notice.

If a neurologist were able to slice open my brain during that time, she would have seen something akin to what a television screen looked like after ABC signed off for the night in the 1960s. Fuzz and static. I kept trying to switch the internal channels but wherever I went, there it was, my fuzzy-headed, cauliflower-looking organ, trying to one-up me, reminding me I was in control of nothing.

I stopped taking calls from people needing their songs cleared for television shows, because the thought of licensing music made me sick to my stomach. And I was ignoring the messages left by my mother asking if I was all right.

During this time, my youngest son came out to me via a very long letter he shoved under my bedroom door one afternoon. I'd known he was gay since he was two years old so it was no surprise. After I read the letter I went to him. He was in his bedroom crying. I sat down next to him, rubbed his back and told him I had known all along he was gay.

What else could I say? I was not very deep at that point, and I might have just said to him, "That's nice, sweetheart. Can you pass the butter?" This was a monumental moment for Erik, and I did not have the capacity to think about what this meant for him. All I could think about was getting away from my life. Mental breakdowns can make you so selfish!

That trip up Highway 395 was the first time I did not feel the pressure of life in the city relax the farther I drove away from the urban decay of Los Angeles. As a matter of fact, being back in the Sierra Nevada only magnified the mess I had made of my life.

I didn't do much when I first arrived. I saw some friends, but mostly spent time alone in the hotel room. I talked myself out of a doozy of a pity party by deciding to ignore most of the voices in my head and go out.

Voice #1: *What are you doing? Go back home and be a mother to your boys.*

Voice #2: *Get a grip! You have a family to support. Snap out of it!*

Voice #3: *Nothing like running away from yourself to help you get better. Not!*

Voice #4: *You hate bars. Just pack your shit and go back home and deal.*

Voice #5: *What the fuck. Go and get laid. It's what you do best.*

Big mistake.

Sometimes those voices are there for a good reason.

There was a place on the outskirts of town known for attracting eclectic and obscure bands from around the globe. On the night in question, a reggae band from Hawaii was in the house. I called a few of my friends. All of them had other plans but I was on a mission. I was determined to go out and have some fun, maybe dance a little. Maybe get laid.

I was in awe of women who could go out by themselves and sit at a bar or dance without a gaggle of their friends close by as backup. Those types of women fascinated me. They represented an aura of confidence I wish I had. So, I pretended.

I pretended I was just as capable as any other Leo woman on the planet of going to a bar alone. I wasn't going to be a Lonely Lucy waiting for something to transpire back in a hotel room while eating a Big Mac out of a paper bag. If something was going to happen, I had to make it happen. I ignored the voices telling me to get back to my kids and instead, got into the car.

When I drove into the parking lot and put the transmission into park, I noticed there weren't too many cars in the lot. Maybe I had miscalculated the dates. I should have turned around, gone back to the hotel room, ordered a Pay-per-view movie for $6.95 and a thin-crust pepperoni pizza from Domino's.

Teetering on the verge of turning around, I heard the familiar sounds of reggae seeping from the building. The one thing about dancing to reggae music is you don't need a partner. I've always loved going to reggae festivals, and it had been way too long since the last time I let myself go around and around to the sound of a Caribbean steel drum and a deep, thick bass. I pretended I didn't have a care in the world, kids who depended on me, or a job.

I made a beeline for the bar, avoiding eye contact with everyone. The place wasn't empty, but it wasn't packed either. Thankfully, I knew no one. I ordered my usual club soda and lime and tried not to notice the tall gentleman sitting three stools away to my right. I glanced in his direction as the soda was placed on the bar in front of me, and smiled briefly as his eyes caught mine. I noticed he was drinking a glass of red wine. I notice those things right off the bat because, under normal circumstances, I tend to ignore anyone who is more than a light, social drinker. Of course, I didn't know if the glass of wine in front of him was his first or his fourth. It didn't matter. I was there to dance and then leave. *Forget about getting laid*, I told myself. I was too tired. I wanted to prove I could go to a bar alone, have some fun, and then go home. Alone. It was a simple plan. No complications. No drama.

The band started up again and I hopped off the stool to join the three other people who were bouncing around the dance floor to a rendition of Bob Marley's "Jammin'." No one was dancing with a partner. My kind of dancing. After two songs, I made my way back to the stool and noticed Mr. Red Wine had lessened the distance between his stool and mine. I was feeling bold. *I should say something.* The adrenaline pumping through my veins gave me a confidence I hadn't felt in a long time. I decided to let loose once and for all.

"You are now two stools away from taking me home tonight."

Why did I say that?

Because I was feeling impetuous and assertive, and working hard at pushing down all the insecurities of a lifetime that had threatened to send me cowering to an empty hotel room.

My words piqued his interest. Within ten minutes, I knew he had a second home in Mammoth and was up with a group of guys for a weekend of fishing. His friends were too tired to venture out for the evening, but he'd decided to go out anyway and listen to some music. The bartender brought him another glass of red wine, and even though he swayed on his stool, I kept up the conversation. I was determined, for the first time in years, to have a one-night stand with someone I didn't know. All the warnings about hooking up with a stranger escaped me that night as I became focused on only one thing.

Getting laid.

When the band took a break I declared, "Let's go back to your place." It had been a long time since I had said a line to anyone, and it was the last time those words would ever cross my lips.

I have only myself to blame for what transpired next.

I knew he was drunk by the time we got to his house. I followed him up the winding mountain road and he almost clipped a couple of trees with his car. His parking job looked like a nine-year-old did the duty.

The responsible voice in my head kept trying to tell me to turn around, but I shoved it down, ignoring the warning signs as I followed Mr. Red Wine's wobbling body upstairs to his bedroom. His shoulder knocked a photo off the wall. He didn't even notice. I hung it back up. He went into the bathroom and came out wearing a dirty white, terrycloth robe, then asked if I wanted to sing Karaoke.

Karaoke?

Not waiting for the answer, he went through the motions of setting up his Karaoke machine. Before I had my bra unsnapped he was crooning to Tony Bennett singing "I Left My Heart in San Francisco." Tony Bennett had never been a part of what I would dimly call foreplay. The voice in my head was getting louder and

I wanted to leave, but being a stubborn Leo, I was determined to complete the task of getting laid.

I took the microphone out of his hand and pulled him by his terrycloth robe toward the bed. He put up a bit of a struggle because he wanted to finish the song. But … he was drunk. I wasn't. He had had more than just two glasses of red wine.

In retrospect, I should have grabbed my clothes and snuck out when he hit one of the many crescendos, since he closed his eyes while singing. He wouldn't have known the difference.

I threw him on his back and climbed aboard. After fifteen minutes, I realized no amount of grinding was going to bring his little partner to life. He pretended to make all the right noises and I pretended not to be bored out of my mind. I jumped off and moved down his body with my mouth.

That seemed to work.

I was wondering if I had enough gas in the car to get home, whether another fifteen minutes of my life was about to be wasted trying to have sex with a drunk, and making a mental note about paying the electric bill when said little partner suddenly unloaded what seemed like a month's worth of buildup into my mouth. Mr. Red Wine promptly passed out while I rushed into the bathroom, coughing and regurgitating all at once.

I bent my head and drank straight from the faucet, found some hydrogen peroxide, and gargled straight from the brown bottle. I threw water on my face, got dressed, and left his room. My pathetic one-night stand, still passed out, seemed like he wouldn't rise to the world again for days.

I went back to the hotel, took a long, hot shower, ordered a movie, and started to eat the leftover meatloaf sandwich I had in the mini refrigerator. I noticed the red light blinking on the hotel telephone, and as I was playing back a message left by one of my mountain town girlfriends, saying that her family didn't make it after all and did I still want to go out, I felt the bile rise quickly from my stomach. I barely made it to the toilet before everything I had ingested over the last day left my body in one quick spasm after another. I still can't get the picture out of my head.

I was up all night and sick for an entire week. On my way back to the city I had to pull over no fewer than five times to throw up. If I ever wanted a cure-all for indulging in a one-night stand again, I had found it.

Did the meatloaf sandwich go bad in less than six hours? Was there so much red wine in the drunk's body that I had a total allergic reaction to the sulfites that may have been in his semen? Or was it simply *his* particular flavor of semen—the sulfite-infested semen of a drunk fisherman? Could it be semen and meatloaf did not mix very well inside my body?

Either way, it would be a very long time between one-night stands.

It would be an even longer time before I stopped saying to myself, "Serves you right."

Fixation Complication

When my family made the move from a town in the flatlands of the San Fernando Valley to a neighborhood located 1,500 feet above the valley, I found myself surrounded by lots of boys of all shapes and sizes, ages, and religions. There were twenty-year-old boys who ignored me when I had a crush on them and thirteen-year-old boys who said things to me like, "If you got a nose job and contact lenses then I'd go out with you." Put those self-conscious memes in the same pre-teen-girl collection bucket along with the scene from the television series *One-Adam 12*, when one of the police officers says, "Girls with glasses get no passes," and my fragile budding psyche took a beating.

Those were the years I started giving pieces of myself away to the opposite sex. But what twelve-year-old girl doesn't want attention from a boy or two?

I did not have a boyfriend in junior high school, and instead lived vicariously through several of my girlfriends in that department. One seemed to always have a boy to hang on to and another had boys to help her be miserable. One had boys who made her write desperately in her journal late into the night, and another had a boy who kissed her and then broke her heart.

That boy who broke her heart? He was the same one I eventually had sex with on and off for decades. For privacy, I will refer to him in this story as MPC: My Pathetic Crush.

The affair didn't start in the seventh grade, but my stomach did do a flip when I saw MPC smiling brightly down at the most beautiful girl at our junior high school. They were a couple, a beautiful junior high couple.

I had posters of David Cassidy and Bobby Sherman on my walls, and I would swear their eyes followed me when I walked around my bedroom. During my teen delusions, I would dream of having a real someone like MPC look down at me the way he looked at the prettiest girl in school, or the way Bobby Sherman's eyes followed me around my room. I was a pimple-faced, glasses-wearing fly on the wall.

But eventually, a fly on the wall with a plan.

I knew MPC would never look amorously in my direction back in 1973, so the game plan was to become his good friend. I would listen to his woes about the girls who followed him around, just like a gaggle of dogs following a bitch in heat but in reverse. I would take detailed notes in class in case he was too preoccupied with his looks to worry about such things. I would become friends with the girls he dated if for no other reason than to find out intimate details of my secret and pathetic love crush.

It was this one compulsion, to track him down through the years, that ultimately became one of the catalysts contributing to my fracture of self. Unfortunately, I didn't discover this little detail until it was too late. Until the splitting of me, atom by atom, had begun and there was no turning back. I suppose I had to go through this pathetic obsession, because the only way you can eventually get out of something is to go through it, experience it, and hopefully learn something.

By the time we moved from junior high into the same high school, we were pretty good friends. My plan had worked. I heard the stories of how he took one girl's virginity and almost took another's. I heard how he had broken the hearts of innocent, accommodating girls along the river while smiling his way through

Spanish class in order to get a passing grade. Girls obsessed over him and teachers adored him. Everything about him was smooth as silk: the way he talked; the way he slowly turned his head in your direction just so he could confirm that, yes, you were staring at him; the way he walked the halls with his slow, confident swagger. He was untouchable. He was loved by all, admired by most.

When he was a sophomore in our not-so-little San Fernando Valley high school, he managed to lay claim to a girlfriend who was a junior. When we were juniors he worked his way into the heart of the most popular senior cheerleader. When we were seniors, he fell into a love groove with a sophomore, mostly ignoring the classmate who had been his constant friend since junior high—me. But all was not lost. At least that's what I told myself.

Sometime between our junior and senior year, I was at his house when his parents and sisters were out of town. I had picked him up to see *Star Wars* but had fallen asleep halfway through the movie. He asked if I wanted to go back to his place.

It was the second time I watched a boy put on a condom, thinking he would want me to be his girlfriend if I had sex with him. I had that "mission-accomplished" glow because I finally had MPC inside of me. Decades later, I honestly don't remember much else about that night other than that afterward, we went back to being friends. So, I waited. Pathetic.

Throughout our senior year, he was with the sophomore, and it wouldn't have been so hurtful if she didn't look almost just like me. She had long blond hair, while mine was long and brown. She wore wire-rim glasses. I wore wire-rim glasses. She wore overalls like I did and no makeup, just like me. I concluded the only reason he was with her and not me our senior year was because she lived across the street from the high school. Every day at lunch they would go to her house while her parents were at work and fuck. I knew this because he told me.

If at seventeen I were able to see things as clearly as a sixty-something-year-old does, I would have opined that the main reason he kept me at arm's length was because I knew who he really was. Deep down he knew I *knew* he was an arrogant, self-absorbed prick. He must have known on a cellular level that eventually I would leave him, because I would have grown tired of his "all about me" syndrome, even though the *me* age wasn't as popular in the seventies as it is now.

I think he invented it.

After our high school graduation, MPC went to U.C. Berkeley, while I got an education about as far north as a Californian can go without jumping across the border into Oregon. I thought of him often and went down to Berkeley once to surprise him. You know, old friends catching up. When I managed to find his fraternity and then him, he was not pleased to see me. In fact, he was rude. I didn't see that then. All I saw was the possibility that MPC would one day realize I'd been the loyal constant in his life, and he would wake up and fall into my waiting and pitiful arms.

He married a girl he met in college. It was around the time I got married on a whim while fishing in the Eastern Sierra to someone who turned out to be more of a life lesson than a right choice.

I contacted MPC sometime afterward just to stay in touch. It was I who reached out to find out where he was and what he was doing. Never him. If the book, *He's Just Not That Into You* were out then, maybe I would have read it. Not likely, unless it was shoved into my face by one of my girlfriends. But I didn't tell any of them about MPC. Ever. Until now.

In the mid-1980s, I was working for a large movie studio while he was working as an accountant near our old high school. I called him. *Of course, I did.*

We exchanged the typical pleasantries of good friends who had lost touch for several years and then there he was, coming through the studio gates to have lunch with me at the commissary. As I tried to focus on the salad before me, I felt myself letting that old obsession surface between the main course and dessert. I had the illusion of being older and wiser and thought I was in control.

For a moment, I saw clearly how it would always be between us, and that I was responsible for all of it. The pattern had been set years ago. I was the one who put the wheels in motion back when we were just kids. My MPC obsession overtook logic, again, and I knew it would be dangerous for me to go there, again, but I didn't care.

In 1992 I moved away from the city for a while, coming back for business, calling him when I was in town. Sometimes we'd connect. Sometimes we wouldn't. It was always me working around his time, his convenience. I wasted precious moments of my life with the ghost of a man who always did what was expected of him and never missed an opportunity to catch a glimpse of himself in a mirror as he watched himself walk by.

When I moved back to Los Angeles after the divorce, it was my phone call once again, announcing my arrival within a fifty-mile radius of his habitat. The affair grew rapidly, both of us sharing thoughts that would have been too unspeakable to say out loud when we were in our teens. The obsession with MPC sparked again, flowing into my life like a virus that would be with me always, never dying until I left this body for parts unknown. I realize now that's what he was—my virus. He was a sickness I couldn't quite shake until everything else in my life spilled over like a cauldron of hot and unforgivable mistakes I had yet to learn from.

He was a mistake and I still, *still*, let him climb inside me when it was convenient for him. Climb and leave. Climb and leave.

When did it start to dawn on me that the fixation I held onto for all those years was slowly eating away at the part of me I needed most? How many times did the universe have to show me signs I could no longer ignore? Was it when we took the trip up to Big Sur for a week of hot tub soaking and drumming? A week so special I was sure he would not share Esalen with anyone else, only to find out soon afterward he took other women to the same place. Maybe it was when we saw each other at a memorial service, and he pretended we hadn't seen each other since high school, when just days earlier I'd let him do the climb-and-leave. Did it start to happen when I realized living an authentic life was more important to me than anything else, and that his façade of authenticity was just that, a façade? I can't remember the exact moments it began to creep up my spine, but I do remember when, after four decades, it finally ended.

I was still numb from my divorce and had been deleting penis numbers from my cell phone when he called and said he wanted to come over. I said no. He came over anyway because *he knew.* He knew for decades I was weak in his presence, and he knew I never said no to MPC. A feeling of dread simmered to the surface when I opened the door and saw him standing there with that smile, waiting for me to let him in. It boiled under my skin. If he saw my indifference and dispassion, he ignored it. But it was there, and yet I still let him into my house, into me. As he entered me for the last time, I knew I was beginning to go through something I wasn't sure I could ever escape. I had let things go too far with too many men. MPC was just a notch on my I-fucked-him bedpost.

I also started to notice things about him I had once ignored: the weird bumps on his cock; the way he always smelled like his dad's cheap cologne; the fact that he always, *always*, closed his eyes when doing the climb-and-leave with me.

I was done.

I try not to be so hard on myself for keeping up that endless fury of senseless passion, because I think everyone should have at least one obsession during his or her lifetime.

But only one.

For the open-minded, an obsession can evolve into a life lesson.

I saw him years later at a high school reunion. I heard his wife had finally divorced him, and he was holding court with some unknown and much younger woman at his side. He never once got up from his corner table to mingle. People came to him and gawked over MPC as he scanned the room to see who was watching him. I stayed as far away from his corner as possible.

It was right after the door finally closed on MPC that my world crashed. Except for family members, I deleted all the numbers of men from my cell phone. I started gaining weight like nobody's business. No one would want a fat Stacey who stopped coloring her hair, and the last thing I needed was to be wanted.

They Wrote the Songs

October 12, 1997 is a day I will always remember. It was the day someone who had been in my life since the early 1970s died. He was one of my many musician crushes, right up there with Bobby Sherman, David Cassidy, Gerry Beckley from the band America, and Jackson Browne. I didn't know him personally, but when I first heard the clear, magical voice of Henry John Deutschendorf, Jr., aka John Denver, I wanted to know everything about him. I was obsessed with his lyrics and the way he stood up for the planet, with his floppy blond hair and his wire-rimmed glasses. I've always had a thing for men who wear glasses.

He sang about truth and love and friends and the environment. He sang about wanting to fly with the eagles, and knew that by living on the land we must learn from the sea. He loved to sit around a fire with his friends and his old lady while passing around the pipe. Even now, as I write about him, tears sting the corners of my eyes. I still feel the loss of this wonderful, heartfelt man.

He had mental health issues that were swept under the rug and allegedly kept secret by his record company. He had suffered from depression for decades—not a surprise if one dissects his earlier song lyrics. He got divorced from the love of his life, Annie, who could no longer stay married to him. Just listen to the lyrics of "I'm Sorry" to get the gist of why they broke up.

I was cleaning the floor in our newly remodeled living room that October when I heard he had died. The television was on in the background keeping me company, and when the newscaster announced John Denver's name my ears perked up as they always did whenever I heard it. The news station wasn't talking about his latest appearance before Congress, fighting for some environmental cause like he did when he spoke out against the Reagan administration's environmental and defense policies. The talking head wasn't announcing how his second marriage was failing, or how he was trying to reconcile with his first wife, Annie.

They were saying something about a new airplane he had been piloting and that he had been in a fatal airplane accident in Monterey Bay. The Long-EZ plane had run out of fuel or he hit the wrong button as he was trying to shift to the second fuel tank. No one really knows what happened during his last moments on Earth. All I know is the day John Denver died, I felt like a part of me died along with him. For me, it was the day the music died.

I rubbed the same spot on the floor repeatedly, tears mixing with Murphy's Oil Soap. I felt the loss so acutely it frightened me. What kind of person mourns and cries and falls apart for a man she only knew through his music? I guess the type of person who was on the verge of falling apart herself. It took only a few pieces of straw to break my camel's back.

I know he had his demons, but so what? Who doesn't? I tried to dump my mental health demons down the garbage disposal with the rest of the rotting food but they showed up anyway, breaking me down. But unlike me, John Denver never had the chance to eradicate his demons.

Even post-breakdown, when I'm having one-of-those-days, I'll find Denver's music and take a long drive, sometimes having to pull over because crying and driving don't mix.

Years later, I was on an airplane somewhere over Montana when I keyed in on a conversation across the aisle. Two gentlemen were talking about real estate in Idaho and Montana. Then the conversation turned to Monterey Bay. One of the men had been on the rescue team that pulled John Denver from the water. In a morbid sort of way, I let myself listen to all the gory details.

It still breaks my heart to think about his untimely demise. If there really is life after death, I hope I'll be in the ethereal audience for one helluva spiritual concert. To me, his voice was of an angelic realm. I wish his angels hadn't taken him home so soon.

Plane crashes took the lives of Patsy Cline, Buddy Holly, Jim Croce, Big Bopper, Richie Valens, and Mr. Denver. Karen Carpenter died of complications from anorexia. John Lennon was shot. George Harrison, Joe Cocker, Dan Fogelberg, and David Bowie lost their battles with cancer. Freddy Mercury died of AIDS. Glenn Frey died of too many medical complications to list. And we all read about what the autopsy found when the coroner opened up Tom Petty after he was unresponsive just days after his last concert at the Hollywood Bowl: seven different drugs in his system, mostly opioids. His heart had had enough.

When one of the musicians I adore and idolize dies, I stop my world and take inventory of what I am doing, who I am with, what I am wearing, and how many of their albums or CDs I have in my collection. I sink a little bit more into the earth and start asking questions about existence, self-worth, and fear.

My love affair with words and music began in the 1960s. I was ten when I put my first nickel into a jukebox, which was located by the front door of some dive restaurant in Kernville, California. We were on a camping trip. My mother was sick of camping food, peeing in an outhouse, and watching my father pull hooks out of trout, so we drove into town.

I was in heaven. Dozens of songs at my disposal with just the slip of a nickel. Mom still remembers me bugging her for nickels to play music.

"C'mon, mom! Just one more nickel," I whined while my younger siblings ate their 50/50 bars. They could not have cared less about the jukebox. I, however, was in love with this machine that could play all sorts of music when I pushed A5 or B7 or G9.

"Leave your mother alone," shot my dad. "We aren't made of money." He went back to ignoring me and took a bite out of his burger.

"Dad, it's just a nickel, and I *have* to hear the song just one more time. I'll rake the leaves in the backyard when I get home. Promise!"

"Oh David, give her the damn nickel so she gets out of my hair, will you? Maybe we should be giving Stacey the piano lessons. She's got music in her bones."

There was no eating lunch in peace if there was a jukebox around. I played "I'm Henry VIII, I Am," and "What's New Pussycat?" over and over and over.

I also got a pink Barbie 45-RPM record player when I was ten. When closed, it looked like a small, plastic suitcase. The turntable was bookended by two speakers. I would take it to my friends' houses, plug it in, open it up, and pull out my 45 collection. My first records were the "Immigrant Song" by Led Zeppelin, "Draggin' the Line" by Tommy James, and "That's the Way I've Always Heard it Should Be" by Carly Simon. Many other 45s followed, engorging my collection. I also loved Hamilton, Joe, Frank and Reynolds and sang, "Don't Pull Your Love Out on Me Baby," until I made the lyrics mine.

When we lived in Reseda, California, my mother would often slide the album *Whipped Cream* by Herb Alpert and the Tijuana Brass onto our RCA turntable. She would take my hands and twirl me around to the rhythm of the title song, or "Bittersweet Samba." One day she made an offhand comment about Alpert attending her high school in Los Angeles. He'd been two years ahead of her at Fairfax High. If they had hooked up—wow. My life would have been entirely different.

I would have been entirely different.

I wonder if, as a writer, I'll ever finish all the stories I have in my head before I die. I wonder if musicians pondered the same thing as their souls sailed toward the light.

Did Jim Croce yell, "Hey! I'm not done yet! I'm just getting started!" The lyrics to his song, "Time in a Bottle," were profound if not haunting. I'm sure when he wrote that song he thought he would have enough time to do the things he wanted to do.

Linda Ronstadt can no longer sing because of Parkinson's. Joni Mitchell said smoking cigarettes ruined her voice (but she did sing at the 2022 Newport Folk Festival and although she didn't sound like she did in the 1970s, she was amazing) and I don't think Crosby, Stills, and Nash will ever harmonize together again. By his own admission, David Crosby was a total ass for years. Stephen Stills and Graham Nash haven't spoken to him in a long time.

I'm grateful Bobby Sherman, Carly Simon, James Taylor, Neil Diamond, Stevie Nicks, Led Zeppelin, Carole King, and Aerosmith are still on this side of the dirt. Even if most of them don't record anymore, just knowing they are around gives me some comfort.

It's no wonder I ended up with a job in the music industry. Maybe I should have tried harder to get a job with John Denver's record label or management company. Instead of going up in a handmade airplane that October day, perhaps we would have been on a business call, deciding how much money he would make if he licensed "Rocky Mountain High" for some advertising campaign. We would have been in an argument because his environmental standards would have gotten in the way of a hundred-thousand-dollar paycheck. I would have talked him into the deal, and it would have been too late in the day for him to fly. He would have had a dream that night, revealing he needed to go up in the plane with another person, someone who would have had no trouble switching on the secondary fuel tank.

One thing is for sure, when it's time for Jackson Browne, Steven Tyler, Paul Simon, Bruce Springsteen, Don Henley, Paul McCartney, Neil Young, Ann Wilson, Bob Seeger, or Carole King to go way over yonder, I know where I'll be, what I'll be doing, and probably what I'll be wearing … if I don't cross over first.

To Bi or Not to Bi? That Was the Question

In October of 1995, I went on holiday with a bunch of girlfriends to Mexico to celebrate someone's birthday. I didn't know the birthday girl but was invited along last minute by another friend, who thought it would be good for me to get to know this group of ladies. I was still fairly new to Mammoth Lakes, so who was I to disagree?

We stayed in a hotel on a beach in Puerto Vallarta, and during that holiday, a few memorable events stood out. The morning we were scheduled to leave an 8.0 earthquake - the Colima-Jalisco quake - shook the entire area from top to bottom. I stood on the street across from the hotel watching the "L" waves move through the town. Marble figurines in gift stores toppled over, breaking into thousands of pieces. Transformers exploded and taxis slid into parked cars. People were screaming and running all over the place. I wavered in the middle of the street, grateful a building didn't fall on my head, holding onto nothing, swaying in awe with the force of the planet.

A few days before the shaker, we were lying on the beach under a palm tree, telling a young man that we did not want to buy an ankle bracelet, nor did we want our picture taken with an iguana. There were four of us on the beach lounging around, talking about everything and nothing at the same time. I was lying on my stomach reading a book. A woman from our group, wearing a very sexy silver bathing suit, scooted her towel closer to mine. Our kids were in the same class at school and she was a bit of a celebrity in town because of her artwork. I looked up from my book and watched her adjust her swimsuit, tie her blond hair into a bun at the nape of her neck, and then look directly into my eyes.

"I had a pretty wild dream about you last night." She said it so casually, as if she were telling me about an episode of one of her favorite television shows, except she was whispering so no one else would hear.

"Oh," I whispered back, curiosity blooming. I put my bookmark in between the pages and met her gaze. "Should I be flattered or terrified?"

She looked at me for a long time. I could tell she was wondering how far she should go by the way she bit her lower lip and tucked fly-away strands of her hair behind her ears. My curiosity was piqued and I asked her about the dream. She scooted a little closer and angled her towel so her back was to the other two women, who were engaged in a conversation about the latest book chosen for their book club.

The dream had nothing to do with our holiday, our kids, or about flying, or finding money. It was a dream involving the artist and myself. Freud would have had a field day with it. She said we were on a beach not unlike the one we were on at that moment.

"We were lying side by side soaking up the sun and there was no one else around. I asked you if you wanted to go for a swim in the ocean."

"How did I respond? In the dream?"

She described how we ran toward the waves and plunged into the water, letting the warm, clear Pacific envelop us both. When we popped up, in the dream, somehow we'd lost our swimsuits and before we knew it, we were wrapped in each other's arms, kissing each other with wild abandon and making love right there between the swells of the Pacific.

"I don't know what happened after that," she continued as she flicked some sand from her arm. "My alarm went off and woke me up, dammit!" We both laughed.

She reached up and adjusted her white, floppy hat, then slid her sunglasses to the tip of her nose and looked at me over the plastic rim. "Have you ever been with a woman?" she asked.

I rolled onto my back and let the sun heat the front of my body for a few moments before answering. I knew what she was asking. "Yes ..." I whispered, taking in a deep gulp of fresh ocean air, then slowly exhaling. "I have."

She said nothing more. Instead, she got up and ran into the Pacific Ocean, her silver bathing suit glittering in the sun right before she dove under one wave after another. I watched her for a while, knowing I could follow her into the water, knowing that if I did, there was a chance I wouldn't be spending the night alone in my hotel room.

I didn't follow her into the ocean that day. It wasn't until years later that we finally found each other in the same frame of mind and then in the same bed. It wasn't as if both of us decided to renounce men and become lesbians. We love men. We had an attraction for one another that could no longer be denied. We are still good friends and laugh about the first time we finally kissed and then got around to having side-by-side multiple orgasms. It was our one-night stand and it never happened again.

Did I miss my chance at same-sex love? If I had been born a lesbian would I have cracked in the first place? Would loving a woman instead of giving myself to man after man have been my saving grace all along? I had my chance. A few times.

As a child, I was very inquisitive, as all children are, about the personal belongings and secret treasures in the dressers and nightstands of our parents. I remember going through my dad's dresser one afternoon. Mom wasn't home and I went about my business, opening and closing the drawers ever so softly. I found a *Playboy* magazine hidden away in the back of my dad's six-drawer bureau. I was shocked, thrilled, and guilty. I snuck into my parents' bathroom with the magazine and locked the door. I remember thinking how beautiful those girls were. Was I the only preteen girl who stole a peek at a *Playboy*? Did that mean I was meant to like girls instead of boys all along or was I just curious?

During my second year of college, I had my first bisexual experience. I knew I wasn't a true lesbian because of how I felt when Lizzie was touching me. I didn't know what I was doing, and it was one of those college experiences that just happened at the end of a long, sexually charged evening.

There had been several of us crushed together in a hot tub overlooking the Pacific Ocean. We were all naked, laughing, all high as kites on some of the best Humboldt Homegrown around. After most of the hot tub water had spilled over the side, we got out and dried each other off. Most of the crowd dispersed to other parts of the house or went home. I stayed in the living room and sat cross-legged in front of the fire, a big blanket wrapped around my body, holding in my warmth.

Lizzie came up behind me and began to rub my neck and shoulders. Being a massage hedonist from way back, it didn't take me long to respond with a series of moans. My body relaxed into her hands and before long, she was leading me into the bedroom she shared with her much older boyfriend. She laid me down on their king-size bed. I remember the blue, velvet comforter feeling soft and warm underneath my back, and I remember Lizzie climbing on top of me, stretching her entire body over mine. It was the first time I had ever kissed a woman longer than it took to say a sweet hello. Her lips were soft. She was soft. She stretched my arms back over my head and squirmed slightly, so her nipples were directly over mine and her knee was parting my legs. I just let it all happen.

The next hour was a blur of bodies, heat, and exhaustion. "Maybe you should decide to come on over to the other side," she purred.

I never did, and it wasn't until years later that I was confronted with the subject again. I was on the downswing from some heartbreak, and a girlfriend who was sick of hearing me wallow in self-pity asked why I didn't just become a lesbian and be done with men altogether.

"One just doesn't decide to become a lesbian," I said. "You are either born gay or straight."

"At least give it a shot. You never know."

I knew. I was born the way I was born.

I know my friend asked me that question because of my lack of judgment concerning some of the men I'd let into my life, but I hadn't given up hope that somewhere out there was a guy whom I could tolerate and who would love me, my baggage, thunderstorms, John Denver, tornadoes, and most important, would not give me any grief because I put three types of breakfast cereals in a bowl before mixing it with vanilla-flavored soy milk.

And what does becoming a lesbian have to do with anything anyway? I take issue with people who judge other people based on whom they love. It's no one else's business! Decent human beings need to be left alone to live their lives the best way possible *for them*. I know plenty of heterosexuals who are hateful, hypocritical morons who live their lives sutured behind a curtain of untruths and denials, bigotry, and antagonism.

No doubt I struggled with who I thought I was during my eighteen-month fall from grace, but I was so closed off to everyone and everything that the thought of ever having sex again with a man *or* a woman was not something I contemplated.

I could barely get out of bed, my kids were screaming for attention from a mother who heard only static noise in her brain, and the stress of wondering how I would pay the mortgage only added to my decay. The hole I fell in was too big. Bigger than I ever thought it could be, so big it took me almost two years to climb out.

Empty Cupboards AKA The Breakdown

The neurasthenia happened when I was walking upstairs to my bedroom. It was the spring of 2001. I dropped my two boys off at school - one middle school and one high school - and inhaled a cream cheese muffin on my way home.

After almost eighteen years, my music licensing job at Paramount Pictures had imploded. I didn't know how I was going to make ends meet, and I was tired of asking my family for help. I felt the walls of my brain closing in on itself. On step eight or nine of the stairs, I halted. My hand was on the wood banister. I staggered, unable to catch my breath, then sat down on the carpeted stair. I was experiencing my first panic attack. I thought it was a heart attack or that my asthma was about to go into a full-blown assault on my lungs. But it wasn't the physical sensations that got me.

It was an understanding that, at *that* moment, if there was a gun in the house, someone else would have had to pick up my boys from school.

The thought scared me so much that I called my mother and told her I needed help.*

Immediately.

I was falling apart. *I'm not allowed to fall apart.*

I needed to keep it together. *I can't keep it together.*

No one in my family had ever fallen apart. *That's not entirely true but no one talked about my grandmother, or my aunt ...*

An hour later, my mom found me sobbing on the master bathroom floor. If I had been wearing mascara it would have been all over my face. Outstanding bills and letters were spread out in front of me, looking like the hodgepodge of a five-hundred-piece jigsaw puzzle that had been dumped onto a card table. In between erratic gulps of air and a guttural scream that wasn't my own, my hands had a minor altercation with the contents of the cupboard. Nail clippers, over-the-counter drugs, cotton balls and half-used nail polish bottles were spread out all over the carpet. A tube of toothpaste had landed in the trash can and a bottle of valium was floating in the toilet. Those empty cupboards taunted me, a reminder of how my well-constructed life had imploded.

Mom helped me into the shower, and while I was cleaning off days of body dirt, she found a few psychiatrists in the Yellow Pages. I was eventually prescribed Wellbutrin and Celexa, heavyweight antidepressants that made me pass the two-hundred-pound mark on the scale and kept me numb for eighteen months.

During my indifferent, apathetic, and mentally shut-down state, I cried uncontrollably for days, ignoring calls from everyone.

I turned a blind eye to what my boys were doing behind my back, unable to engage from my haze of nothingness, leaving them to their own devices. I don't recommend this as a parenting style for teenagers.

I lamented the fact that I didn't like the taste of alcohol, because I needed something to help numb my brain.

I'd forget to shower; doing laundry became a hassle.

I no longer remembered how to cook healthy meals, pouring endless bowls of cereal to feed my boys, not caring if the refrigerator was almost empty. Sometimes I splurged and made

Zatarain's Red Beans and Rice out of a box, but not often. Fast food became a staple.

I didn't give a shit if the lawn was mowed, and let mounds of dog poop gather in the backyard until the stench rose from the grass and a neighbor complained.

I didn't care about anything.

I'm not really sure how I even "cared" for my kids during this time, but I guarantee it wasn't very good. My mother helped and some girlfriends did what they could, but for the most part, my boys were on their own, an absolute calamity and disgrace for any mother with two teenagers. When I should have been channeling my inner warrior Goddess and staying in my boys' business 24/7, I slipped into myself, mostly unnoticed by them. I became a giant faux pas.

Their father wouldn't take them as often as he was supposed to, mostly as a punishment to me, and after a while, I stopped asking and they stopped calling him.

And then the day eventually came when I woke up feeling somewhat like myself.

*My mother does not remember much about my breakdown. Because of early traumas in her own life, as an adult, she's had the ability to forget about traumatic experiences like the one when her daughter checked out for a while and she needed to help her. She has the gift of being able to wear rose-colored glasses during this lifetime of hers.

The Dog Called Cash

In the middle of my inner anarchy, I allowed the boys to go to the animal shelter and get another dog to keep our Lab company. The Lab, Harley, was technically Erik's dog, which meant Aaron wanted one, too. My oldest could be very persuasive.

"Mom, it's not fair that Erik has a dog and I don't," he implored. "I promise I will take care of it. I promise!" We all know how that went, but I was too tired and didn't care about anything, so I acquiesced.

Of course, adding a new dog to a parrot, Labrador, and two boys was exactly what I needed—another living thing to take care of. Yip-fucking-yee-haw-not. Perhaps my guides wanted to save me from having to deal with another responsibility, because the new dog, Cash, was not with us very long.

He was a cute mutt, caramel in color, and got along well with Harley. We had him only a short while before tragedy struck through my own fault.

Our backyard in Santa Clarita backed up to a hill where coyotes roamed and howled. On one of the rare weekends when the boys' dad took them, I had let the dogs out to go pee. I usually stood at the back door and watched them. It was the middle of the day and the coyotes don't usually prowl until dawn or dusk. That day was the exception.

I had gone inside for a few minutes when I heard the howls and yelps. I ran to the back door and yelled for the dogs. Harley came flying down the hill, a peculiar expression on his black face. He ran into the house and promptly huddled under the kitchen table, tail tucked under his butt, his ears flopped down. I yelled for Cash, who did not come. I took a baseball bat and went up and down the hill, calling his name. No Cash.

I called Aaron to let him know that his dog was missing. His dad drove him home and we continued to search all over the hillside. Still, no Cash.

Their father wasted no time blaming me, with all sorts of innuendos and snide comments. "How could you lose the dog?" he said. "Weren't you watching him?"

"Maybe if you would have let him take the dog to your house none of this would have happened," I retorted.

"Great fucking mother you turned out to be," he said before storming off, tires screeching on the road as he barreled down the hill.

It was a while before Aaron forgave me. I still hold onto a bit of guilt about letting Cash out without supervision. That's a horrible way for a dog to die. It was an especially horrible way for my son's dog to die. I should have kept Cash on a leash and let him do his business with me by his side.

A few months later we found the remnants of Cash's red collar, obviously torn apart by coyotes. By then I had a fence installed along our property line to hopefully keep the coyotes out.

When Harley finally passed away, I swore I would never have another animal to take care of. To this day I've held true to that promise.

No goldfish. No turtle. Nothing.

As for the bird? I had named her Miss Willow. She was a green conure with a gold cap. I bought her before my crash and burn, and when I was in the middle of crashing and burning, it became clear I could not take care of her either. I was burnt out.

Simply existing and trying to keep my meltdown to a minimum in front of the kids was exhausting.

Taking care of myself had become a full-time job, a job I was ill-prepared to handle; how was I to manage a bird who screeched every time I put her back into her cage? If she wasn't on my shoulder, shitting on my shirt, she was not happy. I had created a high-maintenance creature who depended on me. I took her back to the bird place where I had found her. I still remember the disgusted look the owner threw my way when I told her I could no longer take care of Miss Willow.

I could not be responsible for another living thing.

Sending Aaron Away

One of the hardest things I've had to do as a parent was to send my oldest son away to a place that was supposed to keep him safe and help him make better choices. Aaron was just shy of seventeen, and it was two days before Christmas 2003. It happened during the time in my life I will call, "The Santa Clarita Years." That time was filled with more regrets than I care to remember.

I was failing as a single parent. I didn't know what I was doing, how to act, who to punish, or whom to believe. I couldn't figure out how to balance my work life in the entertainment industry with my single-mother life. I tried to be a father, mother, disciplinarian, financier, teacher, juggler, and friend. None of it worked out the way I wanted it to—the way I saw it in my head, day in and day out.

In the middle of it all, I fell apart when my kids needed me most. I couldn't function. I lost it. Went on disability.

But you already know that.

My kids had taken advantage of the eighteen months I was under the antidepressant lethargy spell and when it came to an end, and I was able to focus, I saw that my sons had been running their own lives while I had checked out. They were struggling with many challenges: divorce, the move back to southern California, new friends, their dad turning out different than they had hoped, different than I had hoped. Erik had recently come out as gay and Aaron was angry about everything.

My oldest son probably started to morph into the "troubled teen" when he was about fourteen, maybe thirteen, probably earlier. I should have seen it coming. And I would have, had I been paying attention to what was going on around me instead of going through my day-to-day life in a fog with my head up my ass most of the time.

It does happen like they say: One day, or year, your head is in a cave of anxiety and self-doubt, numbed by all the meds you've been taking, then all of a sudden you wake up one morning and say to yourself, "Holy shit! Where the hell have I been?!"

That's when I started to pay attention.

That's when parenting my boys on my own became difficult.

Because I started to pay attention.

I could try and recreate a list of everything Aaron did that ultimately got him into trouble. It could be a handbook for up-and-coming teen con artists and drug addicts. He became the most sought-after scammer of his crowd, and I bought into all of his deceptions and excuses until it was too late. Things went missing and the lies rolled off his tongue with such simplicity and fortitude he should have been a politician. All you have to do is look up crystal meth to know what I was up against.

When I finally flung my self-pity to the side and clambered out of my antidepressant-induced stupor, I tried my best not to let my sons down anymore. That day I woke up and started to feel normal again? It was the same day I could not believe I'd let so much fall by the wayside. Everything had gotten out of control so fast. I was supposed to be some sort of super-mom, bringing home the bacon, frying it up in a pan, never letting my children forget that they should grow up to be good men.

By the time Aaron was fifteen, he had undergone such a change I wasn't sure who I was going to get when he woke up in the morning. Was he going to be the moody, belligerent, spaced-out son or the loving, sweet, compassionate one? He had morphed into a stranger, and I had to do something before he ended up either dead or behind bars for the rest of his life.

Yes, it was *that* bad.

His brother had tried to tell me that Aaron was messed up, and I wasn't doing anything about it. My bottomless pit of hope got in the way of my reality. I should have listened to my youngest son, who was much wiser than I was.

"I should have." There it is again, that phrase. That constant reminder of my neglect.

I got Aaron involved in as many activities as I could. I tried to get him back into ice hockey because he was such a good player. Then something happened at one of the rinks and he was banned for life. No one told me what had happened. I found out much later.

I tried to support his paintball habit but found he had eventually sold all his equipment—very expensive equipment—for drugs. I even encouraged him to try and get into the best high school in Santa Clarita, thinking that being around smart people instead of losers with no direction would help turn him around.

It was a high school within the local college. The competition was fierce, because College of the Canyons accepted only ten out of two hundred applicants every year. Potential students had to go through a rigorous application process, and I guilted Aaron into trying to get into the college program.

"Even if you apply you won't get in," I goaded.

"BS, mom. I'll bet you a hundred bucks I'll get in." I shook his hand.

Aaron got in.

I was proud of him, and hoped that by getting accepted into that academy he would improve his self-esteem, make better choices, and find his way back to me, back to himself, back to being the good brother he had been before the drugs and his anger became unmanageable.

It didn't turn out like I hoped.

All the energy I spent trying to save Aaron was time away from Erik, who really needed me to focus on what support was available for him as a new member of the LGBTQI community. In the end, I didn't do what Erik needed and Aaron got in trouble anyway.

The life of an up-and-coming con artist and drug addict was much more appealing to him than being accepted into an elite school, playing hockey, or being on a paintball team. He was on his own trajectory. Meanwhile, Erik fell through the cracks as I put way too much wasted energy into saving his brother.

Something else, no, *someone* else, was also undermining my determination to help my children.

Their father.

We had a very acrimonious divorce. I found out years later that he had been talking about me to our sons in ways that no father should speak of a child's mother, no matter what. Aaron absorbed everything his father told him. Of course, he would. His father was his hero. I can only imagine what he said to our sons before he abandoned them completely and moved to Thailand in the spring of 2004.

I should have broken the promise I had made to myself to not talk badly about their father in front of them, and maybe they would have completely detached from him on their own.

Maybe.

But sons always have hope that their father won't be just a father but also a dad.

When Aaron was totally out of control, his father was living in a truck somewhere in the San Fernando Valley, continuing to blame me for absolutely everything that had gone wrong with his life since I filed for divorce.

On December 19, 2003, my resolve to do something drastic about Aaron's behavior was cemented by an incident I could not overlook. The wall had come down. It was now or never. There were no more second chances. I had given him hundreds of second chances to make things right, to make his life right.

Aaron came home around seven at night and seemed happy to see me. He asked me to make us some tea so we could talk. Within seconds of my walking into the kitchen to put the kettle on, he ran up the stairs, grabbed my wallet, and locked himself in the bathroom. I had just cashed my paycheck and there was almost a thousand dollars in my wallet, which I was going to use for Christmas gifts for the family.

I took the stairs, two at a time, slamming my fists against the door of the bathroom, crying and demanding that he let me in and return my money.

"Open this door, Aaron! Right now!"

Nothing.

"Aaron! Open the friggin' door and give me back my wallet! That's all the money we have!"

Still, nothing.

Too late. He had already opened the window, jumped down from the second story onto the hood of my car, and was running up the street, disappearing into the cold, Santa Clarita winter night.

He was gone for two days before I finally tracked him down. In between trying to find him, I had been making arrangements to get him out of Santa Clarita. I was desperate. I had to remove my son away from all he knew, and into a place I hoped would save him from himself, and from the path he had chosen.

Again, this took away precious time from Erik, who watched this all unfolding with his sagacious and intuitive fifteen-year-old eyes.

During this very stressful time, I was slipping again. I told myself a thousand different ways that I could *not* go back on the meds which had made me a zombie. I had to be present for my kids. I did not have the time to fall back into that black hole of mental illness.

I had arranged everything within forty-eight hours, including a lie I told Aaron in order to get him to come back home. I told him that a friend I knew had a son who was going into the Army, and that he needed to sell his car as soon as possible. I told Aaron that the guy was coming over early in the morning to show him the car and that he had to be home to see it. He wandered in the door just before midnight on December 22, 2003. I was awake all night.

December 23, 2003, was one of the worst days of my life as a parent. I knew I had failed my son, but I also knew I couldn't bring him back to who he was meant to be. Not by myself. Erik had been right all along. His brother had gotten himself into some deep shit. The transport crew came from Montana at four in the morning. I watched them take away my son, who was screaming obscenities at me as they pulled him down the stairs and out the front door. The ache in my chest was something I had never experienced and hoped to never experience again.

That same night, I had a dream that my right arm had been cut off. I will never forget that dream. It's still as vivid as if I'm watching it unfold right in front of me all over again. In the dream, I was crying and looking down at the place where my right arm used to be. In its place were big, black, long stitches with blood seeping from them.

My right arm was gone.

My son was gone.

I woke up screaming from that dream. It still haunts me to this day.

Years later, Aaron eventually understood why I did what I did and forgave me, but will I ever be able to forgive myself for letting our lives get so far out of control in the first place?

I was supposed to be the responsible one.

I wasn't supposed to let my kids down.

I wasn't supposed to fall apart during a time in their lives when they needed at least one strong, reliable parent.

Forgiveness is a strange thing. Just like the morning I woke up and knew my depression was gone, I hope that one day I will wake up and feel the blanket of forgiveness wrap itself around me for something I wish I never had to do in the first place: let strangers take away my firstborn, hoping that the school in Montana would somehow save him.

But Montana didn't save him.

On Christmas Day, 2017, almost fourteen years to the day when I first sent him away, my world came crashing down again. I received a call from the sheriff's department that Aaron had been arrested. Mental illness. Violence. Meth addiction. More violence. All that school in Montana did back in 2003-2005 was make it worse. Made him worse. We parents never knew how bad it had been for the students who attended Spring Creek Lodge Academy until it was too late.

His father had continued blaming me for everything, stating that our son's behavior was my fault, absolving himself from any responsibility whatsoever. Victimizing himself to the fullest in 2004, my ex said that if I had not, "... kicked him out of our lives," then maybe our son wouldn't have gotten into trouble.

Erik was caught in the blender of all the chaos, and even though he survived, during this time he needed me to be his number one support system, not a mother who blended into the carpet.

Between the Cracks

As a mother, I was supposed to pay attention to everything my kids were doing, how they were feeling, and how they were struggling. Inevitably, stuff fell in between the cracks and got lost. I will always regret how someone so very important to me, my youngest son, Erik, fell between the cracks of our splintered family life.

He was right when he used to accuse me of putting his brother first. From his perspective, I'm sure it seemed that way. Not only his brother, but also his father demanded much of my attention, and was jealous when he perceived I spent too much time with our sons and did not have enough energy left over for him.

Note to my Taurus son:

"Dear Erik, it wasn't that I always put your brother first. He demanded so much energy because of his behaviors and always found ways of bringing my attention away from you. Looking back, I honestly think he was jealous of the bond you and I have. He figured out at an early age that if I was paying attention to him, even if it was because he got himself into trouble and was being a brat, I wasn't paying attention to you. Up until the time I sent him away in 2003, he was always finding ways to break my heart. I did what I thought was right and what I had to do to stop my heart from cracking because of your brother's stupid choices. It took a lot of my attention away from you. I am sorry."

But before the angst Erik's brother brought into our lives, there was their father.

My ex was a working actor when he broke his leg, which basically cost him his career. This loss exacerbated his mental health issues, and his substance abuse accelerated. All of this took its toll; after years of my husband not working, not wanting to find other work, the medical issues, his alcoholism, and his consistent desire to take my attention away from our boys, I had had enough.

When I asked for a divorce, it was censorious and stressful. As punishment to me, their dad would not help with the kids except for a weekend here and there. Those weekends eventually stopped, and when their dad had decided he didn't want to be a hands-on father anymore, I was left alone to be both mother and father to two boys who needed a stable father figure in their lives, not a mother who could barely hold it together.

I repeat: I sucked as a single parent. I had no one to help me with the day-to-day struggles, and since historically my family didn't divorce, I was unprepared for the cards I was dealt, even though I was the one who chose not to be married anymore.

Aaron kept getting into trouble and time spent trying to save my firstborn and correct his troubled ways meant time away from Erik. Aaron was especially close to his father, so when their father spent less and less time with him he started acting out in a big way. I spent way too many hours doing the following:

-Trying to find distractions for Erik's brother.

-Grounding his brother.

-Trying to make Aaron suffer the consequences of his actions to no avail.

-Hoping I didn't answer a knock at the door one day with bad news being delivered by law enforcement regarding Aaron.

Below are just a few of the phrases I used when my oldest was at his worst.

"Sorry Erik, your brother got in trouble again so I had to…"

Or…

"I just got a call from a parent about your brother so I'll be right back just as soon as I deal with this…"

Or…

"A teacher from your brother's school just left me a message saying I have to go pick up your brother because he got in trouble at school for something so…"

Or …

"Your brother ran away and I have to go find him."

Or …

"Your brother stole some money from a neighbor and I have to go deal with that."

Or …

"Your brother stole money from me and now we have no money for Christmas so …"

So yes, Erik, you fell through the cracks.

I wanted my life to stop and rewind during this time. I wanted my kids to not let the fact that their father bailed and their mother checked out have any effect on them whatsoever. I would cross my fingers, look up toward the Heavens and say, "Please just let us all get through this in one piece."

But what I wanted and what happened were two completely different scenarios altogether. Everything unraveled. Years later, Erik would tell me how that entire period in our lives made an impact on him, but he doesn't like to talk about it very much.

I do know that for months he was terrified I would send him away to the same place where I had sent his brother. And maybe, if I had unlimited resources, when Erik got kicked out of high school for smoking on campus a few weeks after Aaron was hauled off at four in the morning, I would have sent him away as well. I had had enough.

Yet again, I was selfish, thinking about me and not about how *all the events* leading up to Erik getting expelled might have had something to do with Erik's behavior.

I had just gotten myself off the brain drugs and was beginning to feel normal when I got a phone call from Valencia High School, telling me that Erik was no longer permitted to be on campus. I had reached my end zone. I snapped. Again.

It was January 2004, on the birthday of the son I had just sent away to Spring Creek Lodge up in Montana, hoping the environment of the boarding school for troubled boys would straighten his ass out. It was already a difficult day because Aaron was gone, and there would be no party celebrating his seventeen years on this planet. After the call from the high school about Erik, I packed a suitcase, called my sister, and asked if I could live with her for a while. I found Erik's father living in his truck in a park in the San Fernando Valley. "Erik just got expelled from school. Be a parent and go get him."

"But I was just going to …"

"I don't give a fuck what you were just going to do. You're his father. Be a fucking father for once!" I told him to stay at my house with our son.

By mid-March, I was back in Santa Clarita.

Erik's dad decided to leave the country to avoid being a hands-on father altogether, but not before bringing drugs into my house. Erik found cocaine in his father's belongings and called me while I was at work licensing music for the television show, "On Air with Ryan Seacrest."

"Mom. You have to come home," said Erik.

"I'm at work. Whatever it is, ask your father."

"Dad brought cocaine into the house. I found it in his bag."

Fuck.

I could not believe their father brought that shit into my home when he was supposed to be parenting our son. I dropped everything and was back in the business of being a full-time mom to Erik while our other son was several states away in a lockdown boarding school. I should have called the cops on my ex but I was afraid CPS would take Erik away, putting him in foster care because of what his father had done in a house owned by me. A lawyer friend who practiced family law told me that if I called the police on my ex, there was a chance Erik would be removed from my home. I wasn't going to take that chance.

By the summer, I decided to wash my hands of the city once and for all. I told Erik we were moving back to the mountains. I hoped by moving away from the place that was the scene of so much angst and emotional upheaval, Erik and I would ultimately be able to let our lives heal.

Going back to Mammoth Lakes was a difficult move for Erik. I was selfishly trying to reset my life and should have considered what all the upheaval was doing to him. His dad had moved to Thailand and his brother was gone. I lost my job. He was expelled and was dealing with a lot of inner turmoil I hadn't picked up on.

The most important being his sexuality.

His brother and father were not supportive of Erik when he came out as gay. I was too caught up in my own bullshit to stop and see how not having the support of his entire family was devastating to him. He was thirteen when he wrote me a letter, explaining to me that he was gay and how sorry he was. He had shoved the letter under my bedroom door and run into his room. After I read the letter I found him crying on his bed. I sat down next to him and rubbed his back.

"Sweetie, I love you no matter what," I soothed. "And we all knew you were gay. We were just waiting for you to figure it out on your own."

"You all knew?!" He was mortified, flipping over to face me. "Why didn't you tell me?!"

Why didn't I tell him?

"It was something you had to figure out. Now let's go tell the rest of the family, shall we?"

Telling me he was gay was no big deal to me, but for him, it was extraordinary. It took a tremendous amount of courage for Erik to write that letter to me and to slip it under my door. I can only imagine how many days or weeks or months he had been thinking of telling me before he actually wrote me that four-page letter. He must have been terrified, and I didn't have a clue what he must have been going through.

What I should have done was make sure he had LGBTQI resources available to him, something he recently pointed out to me. He's right. I should have done more than say to him, "Oh. A lot of my colleagues in the music department at Paramount are gay. Want to talk to them?"

Really, Mom. What teenager is going to get excited about sitting down with a bunch of gay men and women who are decades older than him? I was clueless.

Left alone in the hands of Father Time, maybe one day Erik will learn to forgive me for virtually letting him figure out on his own who he needed to be in this world. My hope is the rift that occasionally gurgles between us will somehow find a way to mend. Like all of us, I'm a work-in-progress and don't always get it right.

In spite of his mother, Erik is a wonderful human and has grown into an exceptional man. Through his TikTok page (@ theglamjew) he has helped thousands of people around the world know that they are not alone, using what he went through as a child and teen to remind them that they too, will survive.

I'm very proud to call him my son.

Not My Tumor

That sunny Los Angeles day in December 2008, when a doctor I'd never met confirmed I had a five-pound tumor sprouting from my left kidney, was, without a doubt, one of the most surreal moments I've had during my lifetime. How many women begin their day going in for their yearly gynecological exam and end the day with the news that a tumor has made itself right at home on one of her kidneys?

Even today, years later, I don't believe it was me who went through the tumor ordeal. It was somebody else. Shit like that wasn't supposed to happen. Shit like that happens to people on *Yahoo! News* or on Facebook or in *Good Housekeeping* stories. It wasn't supposed to happen to a small-town newspaper reporter with a grandchild on the way.

In 2008 I had medical insurance and was finally covered through the newspaper that had hired me to work as a full-time writer, so I made a doctor's appointment. I had been having digestion issues for well over a year, and when my boyfriend noticed a weird "thing" pushing out of my abdomen as I was lying on my side talking with him, we were perplexed.

"What the hell is that?" he exclaimed.

I looked down and saw something poking out from under my left rib cage. It was hard and about the size of a small plum. "Have no clue." I pushed on it, which sort of hurt. "I guess I should make a doctor's appointment with a G.I. specialist."

"Is that the right doctor for this?" he asked. I could hear the concern in his voice.

"Again. Have no clue. It will be somewhere to start as it feels like it's near my stomach."

On December 8, 2008, I had a 3:30 P.M. appointment scheduled for a new gastroenterologist down in Los Angeles. I decided to schedule my yearly gyno exam earlier the same day because I didn't want to make the five-hour drive again before the end of the year.

I have known my gynecologist since I was in my early twenties, and because I did not have medical insurance for several years, I didn't go to the doctor unless it was absolutely necessary, including my yearly va-ya-ya doc check-ups.

As I was on my back with my feet in the stirrups, Dr. Serden and I were talking about the fact that my oldest son, the one who the doc first met via an ultrasound in 1986, had gotten his girlfriend pregnant. I was going to be a grandmother. The Doc was doing his business down below when I said, "You've seen thousands of vaginas over the years, right?"

Dr. Serden stopped mid-exam and looked at me over the tarp that was spread over my knees, exposing the lower half of my body. "Uh, yes, I suppose, why?"

"Does my vagina look like the vagina of a grandmother?"

I had to ask.

He tried to be professional, but it was obvious not many of his patients asked him that question.

He said, "No," the corners of his mouth twitching, trying not to laugh.

Just as he was about to make a clean retreat to another exam room, I asked him to check out an odd hardness I had been feeling under my left rib cage. I figured it was my stomach. Maybe it was petrified fat. I was getting older and couldn't hold in my stomach like I used to. Nor did I *care* to anymore.

As Dr. Serden held the ultrasound wand in one hand and punched information onto the keyboard attached to the ultrasound machine with the other, I watched as the black and white vision on the monitor came to life. He put cold jelly on the end of the wand and made a circle with it over the hardness in my abdomen area.

Doc and I have been through a lot together. Two full-term pregnancies, one abortion, a tubal ligation, bladder infections, several biopsies, my first diaphragm, my first marriage. I knew he wouldn't beat around the bush.

No pun intended.

"This isn't right," he said. "It looks like your spleen is really enlarged. How much time do you have here in L.A.?"

"Why?"

"Because I want to send you over to my hematologist friend in Beverly Hills," he stated matter-of-factly.

I said okay, and like the good little patient I was, off I went.

But not before calling my mother.

She met me at the hematology office located at Wilshire and Doheny. We sat and waited until they could fit me in. When my name was called, they put me and my mother into a small room and sucked over fifteen *ultra-large* vials of blood out of my veins. After that ordeal, which left me a little pale and a lot dizzy, a girl came into the exam room and started to explain blood disorders to me. I guess the spleen has something to do with filtering blood, and if my spleen was enlarged, then whatever it was filtering was making it mad.

The hematologist came into the room and interrupted her oration on blood ailments, saying, "How much time do you have today?"

"Why?" I asked.

"Because I want to do a CT scan." His voice was level and flat.

For the second time that day, I found myself saying okay to another doctor.

Mom and I sat for a few hours in the reception area, reading old issues of *National Geographic* and *Condé Nast Traveler* while the foul-tasting liquid that was supposed to remind me of drinking a banana daiquiri worked its way through my body.

The CT scan didn't take very long, and while my mother and I sat in an exam room the size of a small walk-in closet, I watched the hematologist go back and forth in front of the doorway, glancing in my direction each time. On what would have been his fourth passing of the room, he stopped and asked me to come to the room where the radiologist was reading my scan.

"Your spleen is fine," he started. "But you have a large tumor coming out of your left kidney." At that point, the room got really quiet and my mom put her hand on my shoulder. Then I said okay to a doctor, for the third time that day.

"How much time do you have?" the hematologist asked me again. I wanted to ask him if he meant how much time I had on that specific day or how much time I had left on planet Earth. "You need to go over to the urologist right away. I'm calling him now. Here's the address." He shoved a piece of paper in my face.

I headed back to Cedars Sinai Medical Center on Third and La Cienega—back to the building where my feet had been in stirrups only a few hours earlier. My basic Pap smear had turned into something completely different. It wasn't in my plan to see three doctors at three completely different practices all in one day.

The urologist, Dr. Bui, kept it short and sweet. "You have a tumor the size of a small football attached to what used to be your left kidney. It doesn't look malignant and tumors of that size are usually benign, but it has to come out immediately."

"You mean it's the size of a golf ball?"

"No," he said. "Football. A small football."

"Maybe orange or grapefruit?" I whispered, a feeble attempt at correcting him.

My mother stepped in. "He said football, Stacey. Pay attention." The tone in her voice was different. Scared, maybe.

"What exactly do you mean by *immediately*?" The look the two of them gave me shut me up.

I left the doctor's office in a daze, and spent the next week preparing to be cut open because I had a tumor.

Tumor.

Fuck.

How does one *prepare* to be cut open so a doctor can take out a tumor? Who wants to hear that word in conjunction with something that's wrong with you? Something inside you. Inside me. *Me!*

Fuck! Fuck! Fuck!

I could have dealt with the news that I needed a root canal or had an ingrown toenail, or that my duodenum was inflamed. But a tumor?

I didn't know how to deal with the word *tumor*.

So, I didn't. Not really. Not until I had to.

I had planned on meeting three girlfriends for dinner in Sherman Oaks the same day I heard the word "tumor." On my way to dinner I phoned two of my sisters-from-different mothers, Betty and Lori, and let them know that I had this thing growing out of my left kidney. To this day they berate me because I made it sound like I had a hangnail that had to be removed.

The restaurant where we planned to dine was noisy and crowded. I was the first to arrive and stood between the bar and the small, crowded entryway just inside the front door. The buzz in my ears and head was getting louder by the minute. I was sure I was going to spontaneously combust right then and there. *I have a tumor.*

It would have been absurd for me to have to repeat the phrase, "I have a tumor" several times over the loud din in the noisier restaurant. My girlfriends would have misunderstood me, not catching the word "tumor" amid the raucous conversation surrounding our table of four. Telling friends you have a tumor should be done softly and quietly, as if you were whispering something to your lover like, "You should know I have a mole on the inside of my right thigh." Or matter-of-factly, like when you tell your kids to put away the groceries or feed the dog.

But how do you tell friends you've known for thirty years you have a tumor? There was no pamphlet in the doctor's office on tumor announcement etiquette. Was it appropriate to do it right when we all sat down or after the waitress handed us the menus? Do I say something after the drinks are delivered or do I wait until after dinner is ordered? I didn't know what I was going to tell them when we sat down. I knew I couldn't wait until we finished dinner only to spout out, "By the way, I have a tumor. Can you please pass the crème brûlée?"

When everyone had arrived at the noisy restaurant, we agreed to go next door to the quieter establishment where we would be seated right away.

I waited until after the waitress took our orders and the drinks were delivered. I knew I couldn't get through dinner conversation with the weight of what I needed to tell them hanging over my head. I needed that weight to be lifted and carried from me by these women whom I would trust with my life.

Elyse was to my left, Amy to my right, Diana across the table. I took in a slow, deep breath before speaking, then told them their friend had somewhat of an inconvenience growing out of her left kidney. There was a pause of a few seconds. They looked at me, looked away, looked at each other, then looked at me again.

"You have a what?" asked Amy.

"I have a tumor growing out of my left kidney," I replied, my voice not revealing how terrified I really was.

Elyse, the most practical and logical out of all of us, peppered me with questions. "What did the doctor say? How long has it been there? How big is it? When are you having it taken out?" And then, what we all wanted to know: "Is it cancer?"

I answered as best I could since I didn't know much.

"Dr. Bui is pretty sure it's benign because it's so big," I started. "I'm going to have the surgery on December 18." Diana was silent, taking it all in, then assured me everything was going to be alright. The rest of the evening was a blur and a love fest. Cancer or not, these women would be by my side through thick and thin.

The next day I drove back up to my home in the mountains in a haze. I had to put my life in order before driving back down to Los Angeles the following week, when I would be cut open in the same hospital where I'd given birth to my two boys.

My boys. *I had to tell my boys.*

Double fuck!

If I had received this news when I was in the middle of my collapse, I'm not sure I would have survived. Even so, the ten days between the discovery of my tumor and getting the damn thing removed were very dark. I had to consciously remind myself that it wasn't the time or place to fall back down the rabbit hole. I had to talk myself out of depression—no easy feat when those voices in my head were louder than the ones at that restaurant.

Voice #1: *You've done nothing significant with your life except have a breakdown.*

Voice #2: *Of course you have cancer. Haven't you always done what people expected of you and kept your mouth shut?*

Voice #3: *What about that dream of being a geologist or a professional hunter/jumper? You really disappointed your riding coaches.*

Voice #4: *You should have made your dad work harder at getting rid of his cancer.*

Voice #5: *You've always wanted to write full-time. How's that working out?*

I ignored the voices, telling myself instead that my life needed to go on and that I had to be here for my sons.

At the end of the day, the gastroenterologist appointment never happened, and I indeed made two trips down to Los Angeles before the end of the year. It was the tumor my boyfriend saw sticking out from under my ribs, and it was the tumor that was wreaking havoc on my digestive system because it was pushing against my stomach and various other organs.

"I have the best bad news ever!" said Dr. Bui as he stuck his head into my hospital room. He came in with a clipboard in hand. It had been three days since the radical nephrectomy. "Your tumor was malignant but it hasn't spread. If you had waited another few months we would be having a very different conversation tonight."

The kidney is one of the organs which takes a hit if there is fear, anger, and stress in the host body. In traditional Chinese medicine, physical health and emotions go hand-in-hand. I am positive that because of the constant stress I was under while married to my first husband, my kidney failed. Having a challenging firstborn child may have also contributed to my kidney's demise. The renal cell carcinoma had been growing in my left kidney for years. The mental breakdown after my marriage didn't help either. I had been under continual stress for twenty years. It was a combination of everything which undermined my left kidney.

I wish discussions about mental health had not been swept under the rug when I was growing up. But that's how my family rolled. Serious discussions at the dinner table and at family gatherings were absent. My DNA relatives were great at ghosting anything intense. There were so many elephants in the rooms of my youth I could have opened a refuge in our backyard. Sharing our deepest thoughts and concerns was a no-no.

It might have helped to know growing up that my maternal grandmother was institutionalized a few times and had endured shock therapy treatments. Or that my paternal great-grandfather had a violent mental disorder or that my maternal great grandmother ran away from her home in Lithuania for weeks at a time.

Anyway, I'm just lucky the cancer didn't spread.

So damn lucky.

The Anti-Sister

Of all the relationships we go into and out of during our lifetime, the relationships we have with our siblings can be the most complicated. Supposedly we don't choose to grow up with a particular sister or a brother. It just happens. Or maybe we do choose because there is a lesson to be learned from said sibling relationship.

Being the oldest in a sibling circus of three has its perks, but also its disadvantages. I may have been the first to go to kindergarten, the first to learn to drive, the first to experiment with drugs, and the first to leave for college, but I was also the first to be held up to a standard by my parents and my grandparents, which was as unfair to me as it was to my younger siblings.

I was twenty and on a break from college when I heard, by accident, about the standards some of my family members were holding my younger sister up against. I happened to pass the guest bedroom where my grandmother and my sister were talking about college. It was one of the many holidays we spent at my grandparents' home, and it was not uncommon for family members to sequester themselves in various areas around the house to play catch-up with one another.

I remember the guest bedroom as if I were standing in it forty years ago. Nothing ever changed in my grandparents' house. A twin bed was pushed up against the far wall under the window that looked out over a closed-in porch. The same porch with green

Astroturf carpet where I, as an eleven-year-old, lay curled in a ball crying after my dad smacked me on the behind for calling my brother an asshole because he pushed me into the pool. I wasn't allowed to use the word asshole at eleven.

The crocheted bedspread on the twin bed was off-white with rows of braided fringe dangling from the bottom. The sheets were pale yellow, and the top and bottom of the bed had chrome levers on the sides that moved it up and down just like a hospital bed.

I also got the swat because I made my little brother lie still in the bed while I pulled both levers up simultaneously so the top of the bed went up at the same time as the bottom. He was folded into the bed like the letter V, unable to extricate himself. His scream brought in the adults, who immediately released him from the twin bed prison. I was told to go sit in the corner chair in the kitchen and *think* about what I had just done.

I sat and thought about it.

I thought folding him up inside the bed was fair retribution for him pushing me into the swimming pool.

I didn't really mind sitting in my grandma's kitchen as punishment. It was the best-smelling room in the house. The kitchen was where all the women of the family gathered and gossiped. During a holiday, when all my family members were present, there could be as many as six females bustling about in the small space. Aunt Susie, Grandma Bess, Grandma Toby, my mother, cousin Peggy, and Aunt Miriam would move fluidly around the small yellow kitchen. It was a cacophony of female energy resulting in a fantastic meal for twenty, sometimes thirty people.

I was standing just outside of the guest bedroom that summer of 1979, and could see a corner of one of the two paintings on the walls. They were clown heads created by my Grandma Bess before I was born and before Stephen King wrote his book *It*. I could also see part of the 1930s radio on one of the shelves, which later became a hotly contested item when my grandmother passed away. All six of us cousins wanted that radio, but it went to the cousin who eventually grew up and became a doctor, then a college professor. The walk-in closet in that bedroom was filled with clothes hanging in plastic protectors, as well as a stand-up sewing cabinet with rusted needles and thread so old and brittle it would split and crumble when touched.

I was on my way to the bathroom but stopped when I heard my name mentioned. My grandmother was talking. My sister was silent.

Until that point, I wasn't sure whether or not my sister was even going to college. She didn't like high school very much and was caught ditching class several times, something I never understood. I loved high school. I joined many of the extracurricular activities and ran for the student body office. The only thing I did not do was become a cheerleader.

I tried out once.

Once was enough.

"Are you going to go to college like Stacey?" my grandmother asked my sister. I stayed out of sight, eavesdropping.

I didn't think too much of it at the time and didn't again until several years later. I had no idea what impact a question like that might have had on my sister, but as we moved into our adult years, it all made sense. I found out by chance that for years, some members of my family had been comparing my sister to me, so by the time we were well into adulthood, the groundwork for our non-relationship was already in place. The unreturned phone calls and the excuses she had, one after another for not meeting me for dinner or wanting to go away for a weekend, just us girls. It wasn't for lack of trying to have a relationship with my sister. It was because she didn't want a relationship with me.

I never knew she endured years of listening to other people talk to her about my accomplishments; it's no wonder she spent an equal number of years pointing out everything to me I've done wrong in my life, from marrying the wrong guy to the disastrous financial decisions I've made, and throwing me under the bus to anyone who would listen.

We could never have a light-hearted conversation without my sister injecting her opinion on something she knew nothing about. She never lent me a nonjudgmental ear from her side of the fence, only her illogical reasons as to why my life didn't turn out the way she thought it should.

Growing up, she was told I did everything right, so when I did something wrong, in her opinion, she jumped at the chance to point out my inadequacies about things that had happened years earlier. She was a pro at turning a simple "How are you?" (from me) into a conversation about all the mistakes I had made raising my boys. She would brag to me about how her son Josh, my nephew, would never smoke cigarettes or do drugs, and how he was going to college. She looked down on my boys, who decided to go the trade school route and smoked cigarettes and pot. Turns out, her son Josh is a musician. He smoked cigarettes, smoked pot, and lasted one day at Cal State Northridge. But in his defense, he is a fabulous and successful musician, having found his niche at an early age.

I love my nephew. He's not the one who has been judging me for the past several decades, but he has heard his mother talk about me and my family behind my back since he was a kid. I can only imagine what he thinks of me. Once he turned eighteen, I reached out and told him I wanted to have a relationship with him and that it was up to us. It was going well for a while but his music career has taken off, and I'm sure he has many more important things to do than stay in touch with his aunt. He is an adult and can call me anytime, but I imagine the years of listening to his mother throw me under the bus have something to do with my almost non-relationship with him.

I've heard from several people over the years, many in her inner circle, who have told me how my sister talks about me behind my back. She never had a nice thing to say about me to anyone. However, there was the one time she invited my current husband and me over to dinner because Rod Stewart was going to be there. Her ex-husband is friends with Mr. Stewart, and they often had Sunday night dinners together when he wasn't on tour.

When I was introduced to Mr. Stewart and his wife Penny, who had known my sister for over a decade, Penny said, "Sister? I didn't know you had a sister!" Case closed.

When I finally gave up on trying to have any kind of relationship with her, I felt like the piece of hope I had been carrying around with me for decades finally died. Sadly, I learned not to care. I had always wanted the type of relationship with her that I have with my closest friends, but that's not going to happen this lifetime.

When I had cancer in December 2008 and my left kidney and adrenal gland were removed, she tried to muster up the part of the considerate sister, but it was all a façade. She pretended to care, then started to rag on me to one of my good friends while they were in the waiting room at the hospital, just as I was in the process of being cut open. When my girlfriend, Randee, told me several weeks later what my DNA sister had been saying about me when I was in surgery, I just shook my head. Par for the course. When Randee told me how she replied to my DNA sister's rant while I was in surgery, I gave Randee, my girlfriend-sister, a big hug.

"She started in on a negative rant about you," Randee said. "I told her how inappropriate it was that she was ragging on you when you were getting sliced open."

Randee said my DNA sister continued to brag about herself and her family while slamming me, all in the same breath.

"I'm glad I have you sisters-of-different-mothers to stand up for me when she slams me behind my back."

My DNA sibling did try to be a real sister to me for one year, one month, and nineteen days after my cancer surgery. She called every few months and held back as best she could on judging or lambasting me.

Then I got this phone call in January 2010 from my youngest son. Apparently, my sister posted something on Facebook about his weight, which is a constant struggle for him as it is for me. He called her and left a very heated message on her voicemail, after which the fight between the two of them was on. I stayed out of it. Did I think my sister should have kept her opinion to herself about my son's weight and *not* posted it on social media? Absolutely. Could my son have handled his anger toward her in a better way, leaving out the voicemail full of expletives that my sister would play for anyone who wanted to listen? Yes.

Was it any of my business? No.

It was their war, not mine.

When I called my sister a few weeks after their combat had started, she answered and said, "I have nothing to say to you. Have a good life," and then hung up on me. I called her back.

"What the F?"

"I have nothing to say to you."

"What did I do? I was just calling to say hello." This is the perfect example of her creating conversations inside her head with me in which I was an absent participant.

"You should listen to the voicemail your son left on my phone. I've never in my life been talked to like that. He's just like his father."

"What did you do to set him off?"

"It doesn't matter. He's just rude and he's your son. Talk to him."

"He's an adult and maybe you shouldn't have posted anything about his weight on social media?"

Click. She hung up on me.

I found out when I was almost sixty that her hatred of me ran deeper than just my grandmother asking her if she was going to follow my footsteps into college. Her reason, as told to me directly by her, had absolutely nothing to do with me. Instead, it had to do with an occurrence I knew nothing about involving a boyfriend I had when I was fifteen and she was twelve. Over forty-five years ago.

I had met Wayne the summer before I entered high school. He was the brother of my sister's best friend. When he allegedly molested his sister, my sister also became one of his victims. I had no idea until she told me decades later.

She told me she had been harboring her shame and anger all these years about the incident and directing her rage at Wayne toward me. She said he was my first boyfriend, and she didn't know how to ask for help or what to do with what he did to her.

I felt horrible, of course, finding out my teenage boyfriend had allegedly molested my sister. But for her to be angry at me for decades for something I knew nothing about? For the life of me I couldn't figure out what exactly I did to make her not like me, and it ate at me from the inside out because, well, she was my sister. I wanted a close relationship with her, but she drew her line in the sand. I'm going to need my therapist's help with that one.

I think her not wanting a relationship with me is a combination of several things, but what I do know is that it isn't because I was mean to her, stole anything from her, or treated her inhumanely.

She just doesn't like me.

Period.

But the good news is: I've learned to like myself.

Mastering the Malfunction AKA Not Really The End

Mental illness doesn't just disappear. It can show up in the least likely of places and times. It can make itself known with physical ailments such as heart issues, insomnia, asthma, or a back that keeps going out. It can look like a tornado ripping up the whole caboodle in its path or a monsoon flooding everything within a thousand miles. Brain chaos can mimic being locked in a dark and dusty attic for months, or resemble a conveyor belt of the same melancholy moods over and over again.

At that moment when I was grateful there wasn't a gun in our house, I knew I needed help. No matter how much I taunted, berated, and accused myself of being weak because I wasn't supposed to fall apart, I finally, gratefully, caved in. Of all people, I couldn't believe the big "it" had happened to me.

Now I know better. I know that our brains are all wired differently. Some of us hold it together until the day we die, while others have chronic depression, bipolar disorder, and a myriad of other mental health ailments and addictions that knock us sideways.

I've said this before and I'll say it again: I was one of those people who thought a yoga class, a glass of water, and a good hike could eradicate the funk some of my friends were experiencing. I was 100 percent wrong.

Do I know exactly what caused my A-personality-always-had-it-together-never-going-to fall-apart-self to, well, fall apart? My horrendous divorce and the subsequent fallout was the icing on the cake.

But the cake itself? That took years to bake.

Acknowledgments

To Lisa Lucca and her team, designer John Edgar Harris and copy editor Magdalena Bartkowska. I'm not sure which of my guides put you in my path, but your book editing and publishing expertise has been the best gift ever! I will be forever grateful.

Diane, Koji, Richard, Kirk, and Jarrett, my Mammoth Lakes writers group. You read these stories and did not abandon me. Love you all totally and madly. (Adverbs anyone?)

To the Story Summit gang and mentors. You have all made me a better writer and human. Where have you all been all my life? StorySummit.us forever!

To Sam and Neal and the Mammoth Business Essentials crew. You rock & print and rock some more! Thank you Booky Joint for being the biggest little book store in Mammoth Lakes!

To my boys. Oh, what lessons you continue to teach this mother of yours. I'm far from perfect, and I'm sorry for mentally checking out when I did and all hell broke loose. But at least I bought that microwave so you wouldn't have to eat cereal for dinner every night, and we do have those WWE memories from our Santa Clarita days! As for all the other stuff? Makes me want to put my head in a hole when I think about it. I promise to do better next lifetime if you ever choose me as your mother again. A special love message to Erik: You were right.

Amelia, my lovely and talented and beautiful granddaughter. Your Lollie has lived several lives before she was blessed with you. I hope you grow up and want to know all my stories so you can pass them down to your grandkids one day.

Whoever thought I would be given the gift of incredible stepdaughters when I married your dad that summer day in 2010? Nichelle Lyster, Alysha Lyster, and Katelyn Lyster, you fill my heart with sunshine. Loretta and Calvin, you are the best Oakhurst readers and cheerleaders!

To Bonnie Raitt, lover of short stories, John Denver, Fleetwood Mac, Jackson Browne, Jim Croce, Karen Carpenter, Led Zeppelin, Tom Petty, Elton John, Linda Ronstadt, and so many more musicians. Your music helped me get out of bed during my darkest moments.

Hi, Harriette Powells Spero a/k/a "Mother." Will you actually read this?

Robert Norman, my kid brother. We've come a long way. Thanks for the corrections. You know I love you!

To the men and boys I may have loved before. Thank you for coming in and out of my life. Without you, some of these stories and my inevitable breakdown might not have been possible.

A special nod to Sonia Knoblach. You were my friend and neighbor before, during, and after my breakdown and you never once broke away from me. Ever.

To the girlfriends in my network, especially my sisters-of-a-different-mother. I started to type all your names, then had a panic attack in case I forgot to name one of you. You all know who you are and that you mean everything to me. Without all of you, there is no me. A special shout out to those of you who asked to read these essays as they were a work-in-progress. You are appreciated and loved and, and, and ...

And to my second and final husband, Daniel Lee Lyster, who is always the first one reading and editing my stuff. I know it's difficult being married to this writer/wife. You are constantly amused by my work and a bit irritated when my time in front of a computer takes time away from us. You know me better than anyone and understand me better than I understand myself. I love you through all our phases and am so very lucky to have found you when my "Complex Cavern of Cerebral Chaos" had almost returned to normal.

About the Author

Photo credit: Dan Lyster

Stacey Powells has been a published writer and journalist since 1996. Her play *Stirrups* continues to be produced in several theaters nationwide and her radio show, *The Exhausted Parent Network* is being recalibrated into a podcast. She has several film, television and book projects in various stages of development and works in the music industry as a side gig to support her writing career. Stacey lives in the Sierra Nevada mountains with her second and final husband. When her ass isn't splattered in front of the computer she loves to travel, chase bears off her property, hike, play pickleball, and spend time with family and girlfriends.

Made in the USA
Columbia, SC
27 October 2022